AMERICAN LABOR

America

THE CHICAGO HISTORY OF AMERICAN CIVILIZATION
Daniel J. Boorstin, EDITOR

.abor

By Henry Pelling

70393

HD8066
.P39

THE UNIVERSITY OF CHICAGO PRESS

CHICAGO AND LONDON

Library of Congress Catalog Card Number: 60-7247

THE UNIVERSITY OF CHICAGO PRESS, CHICAGO & LONDON
The University of Toronto Press, Toronto 5, Canada

Editor's Preface

The quest for an American Standard of Living has haunted the American imagination and has unified the working energies of Americans regardless of their jobs. Among the peculiarly American features which have made this unifying notion possible are the variety of working conditions, the high wages, the agricultural background of the economy, and the vagueness of social classes. Because of these unique characteristics it is especially difficult to separate the history of "American labor" from the whole story of American civilization. We must not look for a class of workers but for Americans at work.

One of the many virtues of Mr. Pelling's interpretation is that he is sensitive to these peculiarities of the American situation. After the middle of the nineteenth century, militant leaders of the European labor movements made the romantic mistake of assuming that "the laboring classes" had an international character and that the history of labor in every country would repeat familiar motifs found in England, France, and Germany.

In this volume, Mr. Pelling shows us how working conditions

and labor organization have been shaped by all the circumstances of life in the New World. And he lets us observe how the crises of national life—the American Revolution, the Civil War, Reconstruction, the Great Depression, and the two world wars—have affected the fortunes of workingmen and of their organizations, and how these in turn have affected national politics and the ideals of American society.

Mr. Pelling (a fellow of Queen's College, Oxford) has the special advantage of a knowledge of European, and particularly of British, labor history. He has studied and published widely on the British labor movements and on the relation between labor and politics. From residence and travel here, he also knows the United States well and is at home in the American documents. He can see things about us from the other side of the Atlantic which we find difficult to see for ourselves. He is therefore well qualified to write this book and to help us discover what is "American" about our labor history.

The "Chicago History of American Civilization" aims to make each aspect of our culture a window to all our history. The series contains two kinds of books: a *chronological* group, which provides a coherent narrative of American history from its beginning to the present day, and a *topical* group, which deals with the history of varied and significant aspects of American life. This book is one of the topical group. Twenty-odd titles in the series are in preparation; those already published are listed at the end of this book. Other aspects of the story of American labor will be found in Robert H. Bremner's *American Philanthropy* and in Maldwyn A. Jones's *American Immigration.*

DANIEL J. BOORSTIN

Table of Contents

Illustrations

I

Colonists, Bond and Free

The history of American labor, like all American history, must begin with the colonial period and must also take into account the conditions in the Old World from which the colonists came. At first sight, it may hardly seem worthwhile to examine an era preceding the organization of the first labor unions and remote from the industrial experience which forms the background of our lives today. Yet the society of those early times developed characteristics which were to help shape the future evolution of all American institutions, and in its grappling with the problems of labor supply and conditions of work we can see influences which were to be of permanent importance in our story. As if in the earliest of a series of ancestral portraits, we can there perceive lineaments which were to be recognizable again and again in future generations—and some of them seem recognizable even today.

The earliest settlements on the eastern shores of what is now the United States were made by people who, among other worries, were concerned to find an outlet for surplus labor from their home country. The success of the colonies, indeed, was due in large part to a fear of overpopulation in England in the sixteenth and early seventeenth centuries. As early as 1576 Sir Humphrey Gilbert advocated colonization as a means of easing the pressure; and a few years later Richard Hakluyt could argue in his *Discourse of Western Planting* that "this enterprise will be for the manifolde ymployment of numbers of idle men," and could propose that the "pety theves" with whom the English prisons were filled could be "condempned for certen yeres in the westerne partes." The cost of transporting them to America, according to Hakluyt, would be repaid by the value of their labor in the new country.

And so it was that the settlement of America began, for the benefit of English society and with the support of the English crown. Grants of territory were made either to chartered companies or to individual proprietors, who were thereby encouraged to find the capital for the transportation and equipment of colonists. Of course, there were in the early seventeenth century and later many who emigrated not because of penury but for religious and other reasons. Such persons could often pay their own passage and could maintain their status in the New World as free men, able at once to assume personal ownership of land and to cultivate it themselves and with their families. This was true of the Puritans, who settled in New England, bringing with them from London the control of the Massachusetts Company, and who soon developed a considerable degree of independence. But in Virginia, the other center of early settlement, the first colonists included many "servants" accompanying a few persons of wealth and a fair number "of the middling sort." Furthermore, even those who had had the resources to purchase stock in the Virginia Company found themselves, on arrival in America, to be in the position of bound servants of the Company, whose control, unlike that of Massachusetts, remained in London. In due course they secured their liberty, took possession of farming land, and secured further servants to work for themselves.

Gradually, the supply of labor from one side of the Atlantic to the other and the means of arranging the transportation became institutionalized. In the course of the seventeenth century, crown government and colonial assemblies co-operated to establish the system of "indentured labor," and statutes and regulations were evolved to insure its effective working. The man or woman who was to be transported to America or the West Indies was induced to bind himself or herself by indentures to service for a specified period of years, normally not exceeding seven. The indentures were in the hands of the shipmasters, who could sell them in America in order to pay the costs of transportation. There was no lack of purchasers, especially as it was often the case that additional grants of land, or "headrights," were available to planters who paid the costs of passage for servants. The legal position of the servant was then somewhat similar to that of an apprentice who was learning a trade: that is to say, he was no longer free to leave his master at will and was obliged to work for his master without receiving a wage. In return, he received his subsistence and was entitled *to* certain "freedom dues" at the end of his service, to enable him to live an independent life thereafter. But during the period of service, the master's will was very nearly absolute: women servants, for instance, were not allowed to marry without the master's consent.

The indentured servants were a very mixed group in origin,

even in the seventeenth century, when most of them came from England. Not all of them entered into their indentures freely. In 1662 the mayor of Bristol, one of the chief ports for their embarkation, described them graphically as follows:

Among those who repair to Bristol from all parts to be transported for servants to his Majesty's plantations beyond seas, some are husbands that have forsaken wives, others wives who have forsaken their husbands; some are children and apprentices run way from their parents and masters; often-times unwary and credulous persons have been tempted on board by men-stealers, and many that have been pursued by hue-and-cry for robberies, burglaries, or breaking prison, do thereby escape the prosecution of law and justice.

Among such people there were no doubt many—perhaps even a majority—who had fallen foul of the English law or of English social customs through no fault of their own; and it was reasonable to suppose that the great bulk of the emigrants would become useful citizens of their newly adopted lands. But among them, all along, there was a certain criminal element which was not popular with the existing settlers. The New England Puritans, anxious to preserve the religious code of their communities, were suspicious of newcomers of this type; and, having an economy largely based on subsistence agriculture, they preferred for the most part to do without them. But the middle and southern colonies and the islands, in which a plantation economy was developing, were normally willing to take all the servants that they could get. The limited term of the indenture and the comparative ease with which the erstwhile servant could set himself up as an independent farmer gave a permanent character to the demand for new supplies of servants from Europe, and this created a continuous flow of fresh migrants.

Colonists, Bond and Free

In the eighteenth century, however, the pattern of migration of European servants began to change. In the first place, English economists were changing their minds about the desirability of encouraging migration, for there was a danger of the home country running short of manpower for its now prosperous industry and commerce. It was only the transportation of felons that continued to be favored, and this was regularized by an Act of 1707. Consequently, of the much reduced English emigration in the eighteenth century, convicted felons on seven- or fourteen-year sentences constituted a large proportion. Colonial laws which tried to prevent the landing of this type of migrant were disallowed by the Privy Council, and such was the demand for labor that individual planters could always be found to purchase the indentures. But the views of many responsible colonials were well expressed by Benjamin Franklin, who suggested that as an equivalent the colonies might export their poisonous snakes to England. This attitude prevailed as soon as the colonies won their independence, and in 1788 the Continental Congress passed a resolution

That it be and it is hereby recommended to the several states to pass proper laws for preventing the transportation of convicted malefactors from foreign countries into the United States.

To make up for the insufficiency of English indentured servants, however, a new type of migration had begun to develop—largely from countries other than England. Poor peasants from various countries of western Europe—Scotland, Ireland, Germany, and Switzerland—came over in large numbers, usually as "redemptioners." They signed their indentures, not in Europe but in America, and the length of their service depended on the price they could get for their promised labor and on the total amount of the debt that they owed for their trans-

5

atlantic travel. Because they came over as families, and because they contained few criminal elements, they were more acceptable to colonial society. Some of them were skilled craftsmen, such as those who set themselves up in Germantown, Pennsylvania; but their social advancement was sometimes hindered by barriers of language and, occasionally, of religion.

Without the system of bond service, arbitrary as it was, the middle and southern colonies could hardly have been successfully established. The servants were often quite at the mercy of their masters, and if the masters were cruel they suffered accordingly. Occasionally there were organized revolts of white servants, such as those in York and Gloucester counties, Virginia, in 1661–62, and the well-known Bacon's Rebellion in the same colony in the 1670's. Cases of individual runaways were also very common. The punishment for running away would as likely as not be the postponement of freedom; and whipping was also a possibility for this or other offenses. But this was a harsh age: and the indentured servant did at least have certain rights before the law. He could sue or be sued, and his testimony was received by the courts. For the healthy and industrious, at least, the system held out genuine prospects of advancement in the society of the New World. This is important, for it has been estimated that no less than half of those who emigrated to the colonies before the Revolution came as bond labor of this type.

Servitude by non-Europeans also existed in the American colonies and slowly developed into the institution known as slavery. First of all, there were the Indians, whose land the first settlers occupied. Their number, however, was never sufficient to enable them to make a significant contribution to the labor force. It has been estimated, for instance, that when the first settlers landed there were only about twenty-five thousand Indians living in the whole of New England. Even this number rapidly declined as a result of plague and the breakup of their old society. Such Indians as were brought into servitude, whether by war, by kidnaping, or by peaceful contract, settled down with great difficulty and on the whole proved unreliable servants, often escaping into the interior to rejoin the tribes. Even in the Carolinas, where the largest number of Indians was encountered, the total of Indians in servitude did not go far into four figures and was probably declining throughout the eighteenth century.

Much more important than Indian servitude in the evolution of the institution of slavery was, of course, that of the Negro imported, directly or indirectly, from Africa. Although as early as the middle of the seventeenth century a few hundred Negroes were to be found in Virginia, the number did not increase largely until toward the end of the century, when the Royal African Company established after the Restoration rapidly expanded its activities in the slave trade. By 1700 most of the colonies, recognizing the importance of this influx, had drawn up stringent codes for the subordination of the Negro population to a status distinctly inferior to that of the white servant. The Negro, after all, was always an involuntary immigrant, and there was no need to treat him well in order to encourage others to follow him to America. His term of servitude was permanent and not limited to a few years. Further, he was not normally a Christian, and there was no obligation (so many white men maintained) to treat him as even a potentially equal citizen. Finally, the very color of his skin marked him out from persons of a higher status and so made the slave code more easy to impose.

There were Negro slaves in all the colonies, but by far the greatest concentration developed in the tobacco plantations of Virginia, North Carolina, and Maryland, and in the rice and indigo plantations of South Carolina and Georgia. Although the New Englanders were deeply engaged in the slave trade, the proportion of slaves to the total population of New England probably never rose above 1 per cent. There could be no possible fear of insurrection with such a small group; and consequently the New England slaves were kindly treated, often being freed 'by their masters and frequently converted to Christianity and even taught to read and write. Such generous conditions did not exist further south, except in Pennsylvania, where Quaker influence encouraged a humane attitude. In New York, the white population was constantly afraid of slave insurrections, and an alarm would readily lead to slaves being hanged and burned alive. In the plantation colonies the strictest supervision of the Negroes prevailed. Here they were ruled by the whip, with mutilation and branding in reserve for serious offenses. No slave could travel from his master's plantation without a permit, nor enter into any contract without his master's permission. Marriage was not normally allowed; conversion to Christianity was comparatively rare in colonial times; and, though some slaves learned the rudiments of craftsmanship, most of them were used for the simplest forms of plantation labor. Nor was there any hope of amelioration of their lot, apart from the occasional relief obtained from a kindlier master: their whole lives, and those of their children after them, were spent in toil for the white man.

Colonists, Bond and Free

If conditions of labor were generally harsh for the Negro, and by no means easy for the white servant, we must bear in mind that there were severe restrictions in colonial times even on free labor. This was the inheritance of English Common and Statute Law, which was based on the needs of a hierarchical society and a mercantilist economy. Workers even if technically free were not at first able to travel where they liked, nor to make their own contracts, still less to be idle. The Elizabethan Poor Law, with its obligation upon the local authorities to sustain the unemployed and unemployable, was accompanied by provisions for compulsory labor. Prices and wages were fixed by local regulation, and attempts to circumvent the arrangements by either employer or employee were officially condemned. Terms of apprenticeship were fixed at seven years, in accordance with the Statute of Artificers of 1562–63; and in view of the general shortage of skilled labor, artisans were often forbidden to leave their trades.

Yet rules and regulations could not prevent the poor worker in the new colonial environment from establishing patterns of his own, which differed markedly in different areas. In the largely self-sufficient agricultural communities of New England, there were comparatively few people dependent on the Poor Law, and in the seventeenth century standards of craftsmanship fell, owing to the ease with which the laborer could become an independent farmer. Village crafts grew up, fostered by the long winters when the farmer could do little but stay indoors: but for those who engaged in them, no long term of apprenticeship was practicable. A revival of standards was encouraged in the eighteenth century by the growth of villages into towns, where specialization of labor was possible; and the high quality of public education established by the Puritans encouraged the growth of native artisanship. As prosperity developed in Boston and other large towns, however, it was still the European product that was most in demand, and European artisans were encouraged to migrate to New England to provide the highest quality of goods and services. By the middle of the eighteenth century, Boston was a thriving industrial center in which tradesmen of all types, including silversmiths and coachmakers, found a market for their wares and in which some manufactures, such as shipbuilding and glassmaking, demanded a high degree of organization.

Most of the growth of the middle colonies—New York and Pennsylvania—took place in the eighteenth century, and the population of these colonies was much more heterogeneous than that of New England. But progress was so rapid that Philadelphia, with some forty thousand inhabitants in 1776, could rank as the second city of the British Empire; and New York was not far behind. In the cities there was the same demand for the service trades—tailoring and shoemaking, for instance—as there was in the cities of New England; and the manufacture of the Pennsylvania rifle and the Conestoga wagon (or prairie schooner as it was later to be known) required skilled craftsmanship. The Quakers had a high regard for manual labor, and the isolated Moravian communities at Bethlehem and elsewhere retained a European system of craft organization. Elsewhere, however, standards declined as they had in New England. In New Jersey the complaint was made that "Tradesmen . . . are permitted to follow their Occupations, after having served a Master-Workman not above two or three Years, and sometimes not above a few months . . . ; by which the country is imposed on, having their work done by the Halves."

Colonists, Bond and Free

It was even truer of the South that standards of craftsmanship were in decline. The artisan who found himself in Virginia or the Carolinas was faced by a purely rural society with few towns and poor communications. There was no central market for the specialist's services, although the demand might in reality exist. Thus the dominance of the plantation system forced him, too, to conform to its pattern and seek some way of getting his living from the land. The wealthier planters, who managed to build up a European credit from the export of their staples, could import luxuries for themselves in return; for the rest, they relied on their servants and slaves for a certain rough-and-ready capacity to build shacks and make clothing for the community. As early as 1720 an observer noted this tendency: "The Virginia planters readily learn to become good Mechanicks in Building, wherein they are capable of directing their Servants and Slaves." But if this indicated a versatility on the part of the planter and his bound labor, it inevitably meant a decline in standards.

Everywhere in the colonies by the middle of the eighteenth century the codes and restrictions of skilled labor were disintegrating. In New England and the middle colonies this appeared to be due to the universal demand for skilled labor and the gradual improvement in communications, which put each colony into competition with others in its generosity to the artisan. In the South, it was caused by the loss of specialization due to the plantation system and the existence of slavery. The non-importation campaign of the 1760's helped to develop a new migratory movement from Britain which was to be of great significance—a movement more exclusively than ever before of free, skilled artisans, attracted by the rapid growth and prosperity of the New World and its opportunities for those at the top of their trades in Europe. As Tench Coxe put it in his *View of the United States* (1794):

A large proportion of the most successful manufacturers in the United States consists of persons who were journeymen, and in a few instances were foremen, in the work-shops and manufactories of Europe; who having been skilful, sober, frugal, and having thus saved a little money, have set up for themselves with great advantage in the United States.

As might be expected, the first signs of spontaneous industrial organization in America were guilds on the English pattern—joint associations of employing, independent, and employed artisans. In 1648 the Boston coopers and shoemakers became organized in this way, largely with the purpose of enforcing standards of manufacture and thus retaining a monopoly of the trade in the hands of those who were qualified. Such restrictions could serve the additional purpose of keeping a check upon competition from the newly arrived immigrant, however competent he might be. The guilds established price scales and made arrangements for the training of apprentices, but in the comparatively mobile society of the New World, they rarely acquired much stability or permanence. They were largely confined to the larger cities of the northern and middle colonies, such as Boston, Philadelphia, and New York; and they hardly developed at all in the South.

Apart from the guilds, there were also in the incorporated cities of New York and Philadelphia a number of "licensed trades"—occupations regarded as essential to the public welfare, whose members were licensed and regulated by the city corporations. Sometimes the members of the licensed trades developed a degree of collective activity that clearly foreshadowed the collective bargaining and strike action of trade unions. The best example is perhaps that of the New York carters in the 1670's and 1680's, who complained about "men who intruded into that employment," and some of whom in 1677 were dismissed "for not obeying the Command and Doing their Dutyes as becomes them in their Places." In 1680 some twenty-two coopers in New York signed a "paper of combination" not to sell their casks except at rates agreed among themselves: the Governor's Council annulled the agreement and found all the signatories guilty of illegal combination. There were also various instances of the New York bakers refusing to bake bread when they regarded the prices, fixed by the city authorities, as inadequate. The best-known example of this, in 1741, has been considered the first recorded strike in American history. Like the seventeenth-century instances just cited, however, it was not really a strike of labor against capital, but rather, as David J. Saposs has pointed out, of "master merchants against regulation of prices by public authorities."

On the few occasions before the Revolution when employed workers took action as a group distinct from both employers and independent artisans, it was nearly always to eliminate the competition of Negro labor, whether slave or free. This competition, which was inevitable in the South, was particularly resented in New England and in the middle colonies, where it was by no means uncommon. On the whole, protests by white artisans and laborers on this question were sympathetically received by the public authorities in New England: indeed, they seem to have been an important factor in the abolition of slavery there. In the South, where the Negro population was large, the most that could be done was to limit the employment of Negroes in skilled trades.

Perhaps the nearest thing to a labor strike in the prerevolutionary period was the action of the Negro chimney sweeps in Charleston in 1761. It was reported that they "had the insolence, by a combination among themselves, to raise the usual prices, and to refuse doing their work, unless their exorbitant demands are complied with." This, certainly, was something that the slaves on the plantations were never in a position to do. For them, as for the indentured servant, the only effective form of protest seemed to be either the collective rebellion or the individual act of running away. Southern newspapers testify to the large number of servants and slaves who took the latter course. As for rebellions by slaves, compared with revolts by indentured servants they were rare before the eighteenth century. Only as the number of slaves increased and as they became more familiar with their surroundings and their fellow slaves did they begin to resort more frequently to such drastic and dangerous action.

How far can we discover distinctive characteristics of American labor as a whole in the prerevolutionary period? Clearly there were enormous differences of standards and conditions of life, ranging from the independence and prosperity of the skilled craftsman in the northern cities to the closely regulated drudgery of many Negro slaves on the plantations. But this very fact of diversity was to be an American characteristic. It was partly a result of geographical differences between one region and another, which caused differences of economy and hence of social structure. But it was also a product of the varying origins of the workers themselves and their status when they or their forebears crossed the Atlantic. Out of this heterogeneity it was difficult for any class-consciousness to emerge, even in the towns where craftsmen and laborers were beginning in the eighteenth century to congregate in some numbers. As Carl Bridenbaugh has observed, if one attempts to draw a line of division between manual workers and others on a scale of wealth and social standing, the line must be drawn not horizontally but vertically. But, at the same time, the difference of status between all white workers and Negroes was already becoming very marked, and it was a difference that the white worker was as a rule very anxious to emphasize.

The second most important characteristic of American labor in this period was the closeness of its ties with agriculture and the ease with which, owing to the ready access to unclaimed land, the free laborer could set himself up as an independent farmer. In every section, agriculture was overwhelmingly the predominant occupation, and the white servant knew that after completing his indentures it was possible for him to move to the frontier to claim land for himself. Contemporaries were fully aware of the importance of the link between the existence of free land and the social and economic status of both free and bond labor. As Benjamin Franklin put it in 1751, "Till it is fully settled, Labour will never be cheap here, where no Man continues long a labourer for others, but gets a Plantation of his own, no Man continues long a Journeyman to a Trade, but goes among those new Settlers and sets up for himself. . . ." Such a state of affairs, Franklin realized, was paradoxically responsible also for perpetuating the system of indentured labor as a way of securing fresh immigrants: "The labour of the plantations is performed chiefly by indentured servants brought from Great Britain, Ireland and Germany, because the high price it bears cannot be performed in any other way." But the initial disadvantage of being indentured, as he pointed out, did not prevent these people from bettering themselves in a way which would hardly ever have been open to them in Europe. It was the Negro alone who obtained no advantage from the existence of free land, for the shortage of labor on the plantations only served to rivet more securely upon him the chains of his servitude. Already by the end of the colonial period the Negro had become the great exception to the generalization that immigration to America not only tended to improve the lot of the worker but also enabled him to rise rapidly in social status.

The third most important characteristic, not unrelated to the others, was the relatively high rate of wages which prevailed for all free labor in the colonies. In spite of all attempts to regulate wages, it was generally reckoned that the American rate was anything from 30 to 200 per cent higher than that current in England. As early as 1639 John Winter could write from Maine that if existing wage rates continued, "the servants will be masters and the masters servants"; and a few years later the estimate was made that labor in New England was "ordinarily as much again as in England, and in many things treble." After more than a century had passed Crèvecœur, looking at it from the farmer's point of view, could write:

As to labour and labourers,—what a difference! When we hire any of these people we rather pray and entreat them. You must give them what they ask: three shillings per day in common wages and five or six shillings in harvest. They must be at your table and feed, as you saw it at my house, on the best you have. I have often seen Irishmen just landed, inconceivably hard to please and as greedy as wolves. . . . Our mechanics and tradesmen are very dear and sometimes great bunglers. . . .

Of course, wages had to be higher in America or there would have been no incentive for migration: the premium was, in fact, largely imposed by distance from the best supplies of labor. But in a frontier society, as Crèvecœur indicated, it carried with it also a freedom of manners impossible in Europe: ". . . they must be at your table and feed." This was a characteristic to be noted, usually with aversion, by a succession of upper-class travelers from Europe in the course of American history.

All these characteristic lineaments, as we have called them, may be seen if we look at the pattern of American society at the time of the Revolution. It used to be maintained that the Revolution determined not only whether Americans should have home rule but also who was to rule at home—in other words, that there was a social revolution accompanying the struggle against the British crown. More recent research has shown, however, that in many of the colonies the franchise already extended to a large proportion of the adult male population and that property ownership was widely diffused. This was true, at least, of Massachusetts and probably of several of the other colonies. In fact, it is not easy to pick out those colonies where significant social conflicts did occur at the time of the Revolution. Probably the best example is Pennsylvania, where the issue was between a narrow oligarchy of Philadelphia merchants on the one side and, on the other, a mixed alliance of artisans, lesser merchants, and upstate farmers. Everywhere, the "mechanics" constituted too small a minority to effect a revolution by themselves, even had they wanted to; and in the countryside there was no large class of landless laborers, as in England, or peasants oppressed by feudal dues, as in France, but rather a great variety of independent farmers.

American Labor

The most active citizens in the towns formed themselves into organizations known as the "Sons of Neptune" and the "Sons of Liberty," with the intention of working for freedom from British control; and the fact that these bodies contained a predominance of seamen and mechanics has led some to conclude that they were instruments of social revolution. But the societies put forward no program suggesting class grievances, and those who were free men probably had little sense of class inferiority. Even in Pennsylvania, where the closest approach to a genuine social conflict existed, the situation was well summed up in a local paper as follows:

The People of this Province are generally of the middling Sort, and at present pretty much upon a level. They are chiefly industrious Farmers, Artificers or Men in Trade, they enjoy and are fond of Freedom, and the *meanest among them* thinks he has a right to Civility from the greatest.

It remains true that the urban workers were the readiest to take the lead in disturbances in the Revolutionary period. They were, after all, the obvious nucleus of any mob or band of angry citizens, for such bodies are more likely to collect in the towns than in the countryside. The seamen among them resented the treatment that they received at the hands of the Royal Navy, and the urban workers on occasion, as at Boston, found the British soldiers competing for their jobs on a temporary basis. The workers also probably thought that they stood to gain by the non-importation agreements; and so they were willing enough to withstand the blandishments of General Gage, who wanted to build his fortifications with local labor. When the time came, they enlisted in considerable numbers in the Revolutionary armies and joined in the task begun by the "embattled farmers" of Concord. Indentured servants

This Indenture MADE the *Thirtyeth* Day of *April* in the Year of our LORD one thousand seven hundred and *Seventy four* BETWEEN *John Buchanan Wᵐ Monison & Co* of the one Part, and

Joobell Smith of the other Part, WITNESSETH, that the said *Joobell Smith* doth hereby covenant, promise, and grant, to and with the said *John Buchanan Wᵐ Monison & Co* their Executors, Administrators, and Assigns, from the Day of the Date hereof, until the first and next Arrival at *Newyork* in *America*, and after for and during the Term of *Three* Years, to serve in such Service and Employment as the said *J Buchanan Wᵐ Monison & Co* or their Assigns shall there employ *her* according to the Custom of the Country in the like Kind. In Consideration whereof, the said *J Buchanan Wᵐ Monison & Co* doth hereby covenant and grant to and with the said *Joobell Smith* to pay for *her* Passage, and to find and allow *her* Meat, Drink, Apparel, and Lodging, with other Necessaries, during the said Term; and at the End of said Term to pay unto *her* the usual Allowance, according to the Custom of the Country in the like Kind. ~~PROVIDED always, that if the said shall pay, or cause to be paid, unto the said or his Assigns, the Sum of Currency in Days next after Arrival at aforesaid; then these Presents to be void, otherwise to remain in full Force.~~ IN WITNESS whereof, the Parties above-mentioned to these Indentures, have interchangeably put their Hands and Seals, the Day and Year first above-written.

Signed, sealed, and delivered, } *John Buchanan Wᵐ Monison* in the Presence of *& Co*

John Brodie
Arch Brown　　　*Joobell ᵸᵉʳ Smith*

These are to Certify That the above named Joabella Smith Came before me, Notary Publick Subscribing Duely admitted & Sworn Residing in Gacenock in the County of Renfrew North Brittain this Fourteenth Day of May and year abovementioned and Declared herself to be of the Age of Ninteen years and as covenanted or contracted Servant to any other person or persons than the above named Messᵈ John Buchanan William Monison & Co and that she Voluntarly & her own Accord Signed this Indenture and was no ways Coaded or Compelled thereto.

John Moody Nᵖ

Indenture of a Scottish servant girl, 1774. (Courtesy, Chicago Historical Society.)

Advertisement of a slave sale, 1856. The prices fetched are penciled in. (Courtesy, Chicago Historical Society.)

who enlisted were promised their liberty; and although this caused some friction between their masters and the military authorities, many of them were able to take the opportunity thus afforded of joining private advantage with the national cause.

As might be expected, the Negro found it difficult to associate his own welfare with the Revolutionary cause. At first, many slaves took advantage of the disorder to escape, and often to desert to the British—a course that rarely proved of advantage, for it did not lead to emancipation but rather to continued service and often to resale in the West Indies. In the North, where free Negroes were not uncommon, many volunteered for service with the Revolutionary armies and were eventually accepted into the ranks, although with some hesitation on the part of the Continental Congress. In the South, however, some of the colonies forbade the enlistment of Negroes.

Yet the Revolution was not without social consequences, many of them tending to improve the position of the worker, especially of the worker not yet free. The enunciation of the principles of individual liberty and equality, even if qualified by the recognition of existing institutional limitations, had clear implications for the future status of both servant and slave. White servitude was already in decline, largely owing to the difficulties of transportation and supply, which increased whenever Europe was at war. Slavery was in fact abolished in New England in the immediately succeeding years; and by the Northwest Ordinance it was forbidden in the territories north of the Ohio River. In the middle colonies the institution disappeared more gradually, but hardly survived into the nineteenth century. Although it persisted in the South, where of course the great bulk of the slaves had always been, there was nevertheless a widespread impression that, like indentured servitude, it would inevitably disappear as the nation increased its domestic resources of labor in succeeding generations. What with the sale of the large Tory estates, the reform of inheritance laws, and the abolition of restrictions on landownership and westward expansion, at the end of the eighteenth century the American people seemed far along the path of social equality.

II

Social Experiments and the Problem of Slavery

The years from the achievement of independence to the beginning of the Civil War present a certain unity for the historian of labor. They form a period of very extensive expansion of the national domain and of much migration beyond the bounds of the former colonies—the latter, however, more than offset by the natural increase of the population and by an ever growing, fresh immigration from Europe. Communications rapidly improved, markets widened, and in spite of competition from Britain and other parts of Europe, manufacturing industry began to develop, especially in New England and around New York and Philadelphia. Yet it could not be said that the effects of these changes as yet dominated the American scene: only a small proportion of those engaged in industry became concentrated in factories before the Civil War; and in any case, agriculture remained by far the dominant occupation of the country. The improvement of communications and the widening of markets helped to increase a sense of nationality, especially in the West; but differences remained between the North and South, whose growing estrangement led in the end to the outbreak of the Civil War in 1861.

At the end of the eighteenth century, many of those who looked to the future were for keeping the industrial revolution altogether out of the United States, so that the country would remain almost exclusively agricultural. The writings of Alexander Hamilton and of his assistant at the Treasury, Tench Coxe, assumed an apologetic tone when they pleaded for the establishment of more industrial undertakings. It was felt that the introduction of manufacturing in a concentrated form and on a large scale would deprive the farmers of the already very limited supplies of labor at their disposal; and at the same time there was much doubt whether the United States could compete effectively with Great Britain, where labor was cheaper, where skilled craftsmen were less scarce, and where capital was more readily available. These hesitations, moreover, were associated with a belief, partly derived from the European experience, that factory work was harmful and degrading to those who engaged in it and that agriculture was the only satisfactory basis for a stable and generally equalitarian society.

To deal with these arguments, Hamilton and Coxe were at pains to point out that a certain amount of industry could well be sustained by the United States without any diminution of the existing concentration upon agriculture, provided that the latest labor-saving devices were employed, and provided also that the labor force were recruited in large part either from immigrants or from the wives and children of the farmers themselves, who could thus supplement the agricultural earnings of their men. "The husbandman himself," said Hamilton, "experiences a new source of profit and support from the increased industry of his wife and daughters, invited and stimulated by the demands of the neighbouring manufactories."

At the time that Hamilton was writing, certain trades, it is true, were already necessarily being undertaken on a large scale; the most important of them were probably shipbuilding, iron manufacture, and brewing. But industry as a whole was still largely a matter of household work, supplemented as necessary by the skill of craftsmen, many of them itinerant, others living in the towns and making goods to order for individual patrons. According to Tench Coxe, in 1787 the total population of New England engaged in all forms of industry—including fisheries, navigation, and trade—was only one-eighth of the total engaged in agriculture. For other parts of the Union, it was considerably less.

The rapid growth of the American population from four million in 1790 to thirty-one million in 1860, coupled with the improvement of transportation in the early nineteenth century—especially the construction of canals and railroads—enormously expanded the domestic market for manufactured goods and, in spite of strong competition from British exporters, provided great opportunities for American enterprise. This caused a revolution in the methods of production, even in industries which could not as yet be adapted to the use of power-driven machinery. The primacy of custom or "bespoke" work for local markets by individual craftsmen was replaced by a concentration upon the output of wholesale goods for a wider and more remote demand. This type of large-scale manufacture could only be organized in a factory if suitable machinery was available; otherwise, it necessitated the development of an intensified "putting-out" system. Thus, whereas in colonial times boots and shoes had been made at home by the farmer himself, perhaps with the assistance of an itinerant cobbler, or had been specially ordered by individual patrons, it now became normal throughout the nation, even in the South, for "store shoes" to be bought indirectly from large-scale manufacturers in New England. These "store shoes" were not quite as good as custom-made shoes: but by a process of subdivision of labor they could be produced more quickly and with less highly skilled craftsmen. As a result the individual shoemaker lost his independence to the merchant-capitalist who could organize the trade on this basis; and his standard of skill and his rate of wages both tended to decline.

It was in the textile industries that power-driven machinery was first employed after the pattern of developments in England; and machinery transformed methods of production in a still more remarkable fashion. A cotton industry based upon water power began to develop around the turn of the century in Rhode Island and in Massachusetts, north of Boston. The two areas have to be distinguished, because they developed somewhat different industrial systems. That north of Boston depended, as Hamilton had suggested, on the work of women from the New England farms. In practice they were usually the young unmarried girls, who came to spend a short season of their lives in independent wage-earning, and who were accommodated in "model" lodging-houses erected by the management. This was the celebrated "Lowell system," much admired by visitors from far and wide, owing to the apparent intelligence, culture, and good health of its operatives. The Rhode Island system, on the other hand, developed more on the English plan of employing whole families—men as well as women and children—with little or no supervision of their home life. These two areas contained the great bulk of the early American cotton industry, but there were also some establishments at Paterson, New Jersey, and near Philadelphia. A woolen industry based on power-driven machinery grew up on similar lines, and in much the same districts, although progress was somewhat slower. In both cotton and wool, indeed, handloom weaving continued to be important until the middle of the century.

The growth of the factory system beyond the textile industries took place only quite late in the period that we are considering. It was largely the result of the standardization of processes of manufacture, so that interchangeable parts could be made for complicated products. Much of the credit for developing the method is usually given to Eli Whitney, who first introduced it for the manufacture of small arms. About the middle of the century it began to be applied to the manufacture of clocks and watches, locks, agricultural implements, and sewing machines. Many of these products, which could now be made by comparatively unskilled operatives, replaced imported goods which were still made by the application of the highest skills. By the time of the International Exhibition in London in 1851, American industry could show many devices and processes which were technically in advance of those used in Britain; and European technical experts suddenly realized that they had much to learn from their transatlantic competitors. This was all the more remarkable in view of the small scale of American industry at this time, whether in proportion to British industry or in proportion to the size of the United States itself. By 1860 one in eight of the New England population was engaged in some manufacturing industry (not necessarily factory industry, however); but elsewhere it was very substantially less—one in fifteen in the middle states, one in forty-eight in the West, and only one in eighty-two in the South. Thus in spite of her rapid industrial development, the United States remained, as we have already suggested, a predominantly agricultural nation in the period before the Civil War.

In spite of the absence of guilds and the comparative weakness of apprenticeship in the United States, the working class or classes of the early national period contained at the outset a clearly marked "aristocracy" of skilled artisans. There were, for instance, the printers, the carpenters, the shoemakers or cordwainers, and the tailors; and we find that each of these groups was able to form trade societies in the 1790's or early in the nineteenth century. Of course, these bodies were at first entirely local in character, based upon individual cities or towns and not extending beyond them except into the immediate countryside; for as yet the great widening effect of the revolution in transportation had not taken place. Their objects, in the first instance, were as much to provide their members with mutual insurance benefits and social advantages as to protect the employees or journeymen against the employers or masters. In fact, master craftsmen and independent artisans often belonged to these bodies in the early years of their existence and ceased to belong to them only as methods of organization changed and created sharp conflicts of economic interest between employer and employed. When this happened, the trade societies assumed directly industrial functions; they sought to bargain with the masters on behalf of the journeymen, and, if they secured no satisfaction, they not infrequently organized strike action against the masters.

It appears that the "first continuous organization of wage-earners for the purpose of maintaining or advancing wages" (to quote a definition used by David J. Saposs) was a society of shoemakers at Philadelphia, founded in 1792. This body, which collapsed and had to be reorganized in 1794, stayed in existence until 1806. In 1794 the printers of New York City founded a Typographical Society, and in the following score of years several societies of shoemakers and printers sprang up in other cities. These two trades were apparently alone in establishing permanent trade societies in these years; organizations of other trades that we hear of, such as the Philadelphia carpenters and the Baltimore tailors, did not last. The general lack of permanence was probably due in part to the efforts made by the masters to initiate prosecutions of their members for "conspiracy" and the willingness of the courts to sustain these prosecutions.

The initially defensive purpose of the trade societies is clearly shown by an examination of the grievances that their spokesmen enumerated: their aim was to maintain, rather than to advance, existing wages and conditions. Often, of course, their grievances were directed as much against their fellow workmen as against the employers. The New York Typographers, for instance, complained of the practice of

taking full grown men (foreigners) as apprentices for some twelve or fifteen months, when they are to be turned into the situations of men who are masters of their business, which men are to be turned out of their places by miserable botchers because they will work for what they can get.

Similarly, the New York shoemakers deplored the large number of apprentices in their shops and maintained that "two

American Labor

was as many as one man could do justice by." The societies
sought to safeguard their members' interests against the threat
of competition by poorly trained workmen, but, as we have
seen, the long-term trend of economic evolution was likely to
run against them.

These early unionists soon learned what we would regard
as the essential tactics of strike action, and a little more besides.
They did not always give strike benefits to their members,
but sometimes sustained them by what were described as loans
for the needy. The strikes were not always peaceful, and in
the one which gave rise to the first famous conspiracy case
—the strike of the Philadelphia Cordwainers in 1806—"scabs"
were attacked, and hostile employers had their shop windows
broken. The boundaries of legitimate and illegitimate action
were of course hard to find at a time when special trade-union
legislation did not exist, and when the artisans' need to combine came into open conflict with the old common law of
"conspiracy in restraint of trade." As time went on, indeed,
public opinion began to cause a change in the emphasis of
prosecutions, without any lead either from the judges or from
the legislatures. The simple issue of combination was put aside,
and prosecutions came to be based increasingly upon allega-
tions of illegality in the methods used by the societies to enforce their position. It was, after all, easier to convince a jury
that intimidation or coercion were to be condemned than that
the act of combining was in itself a bad thing. This common-
sense attitude finally received confirmation from the bench
in the well-known Massachusetts case of *Commonwealth* v.
Hunt (1842). In the meantime, however, the years of depression after the end of the War of 1812 caused widespread un-

employment, and the early trade societies were all of them swept out of existence.

With the return of more prosperous times in the 1820's a new expansion of unionism took place, and a wider range of trades was involved. Factory operatives, however, most of whom were women and children, did not participate in this revival of activity. The main interest of many of the artisans seems to have been in securing a reduction of their hours of work, which up to this time customarily ran "from sunrise to sunset." In 1825 there was a successful strike of Boston house carpenters on the issue; and in New York City the demand for a ten-hour day was put forward by skilled workers in many trades and for the most part accepted by the employers. Efforts with the same object at Philadelphia led in 1827 to a new development of organization—the formation of a city federation of trade societies known as the Philadelphia Mechanics Union of Trade Associations.

Gradually and locally, therefore, the artisans were bringing pressure to bear to improve their industrial conditions; and in periods of good trade they made a few limited gains. But at the same time, with the growing wealth of other sections of society, it is not surprising that they felt that their relative position was deteriorating. This feeling, more than anything else, was responsible for their sudden interest in attempting to achieve social aims by political activity. It coincided with a widening of the franchise in many states, to include, if not all adult white males, at any rate all taxpayers. As a result, "workingmen's parties" appeared in many cities and towns at the end of the 1820's. Their programs were for the most part remarkably uniform. They demanded universal free public education, so that the inferiorities of economic status would not inevitably be transferred to their children. They also voiced strong opposition to the widespread extension of banking privileges by state action, which they thought was responsible for the financial crises and depressions, and the decline in the value of money from which they had suffered. They urged the abolition of imprisonment for debtors; changes in the militia law, which bore heavily on the workingman; and a mechanics' lien law, which would give the employee priority in the payment of his wages in cases of default by an employer.

The two most important of these workingmen's parties—that of Philadelphia, which initiated the whole movement in 1828, and that at New York which came into existence the following year—were to a certain extent under the influence of theorists who advocated revolutionary change of one sort or another. At Philadelphia there was William Heighton, a shoemaker who derived some of his ideas from the early British Socialists; and at New York there was a whole range of propagandists varying from Thomas Skidmore, the proponent of a leveling philosophy based on Jefferson and Paine, and George Henry Evans, the land reformer, to the redoubtable Scottish utopians Robert Dale Owen and Frances Wright. In general, however, these radicals failed to win control of movements that were essentially conservative-reformist in character. Both at Philadelphia and at New York workingmen's candidates won some successes at elections in 1830, but factionalism and the eagerness of both Whigs and Democrats to bid for their support led to their formal disintegration before the 1832 elections.

Social Experiments and Problem of Slavery

The New England Association of Farmers, Mechanics and Other Workingmen, which came into existence in 1831 and lasted for some three years, owed its origin to the ten-hour agitation. It went into politics in Massachusetts, drawing much of its support from the countryside rather than from the towns. By themselves the factory workers, who were so largely drawn from farming families, and who were mostly women and children, did not constitute an effective political group. The Association's urban supporters, who were not particularly numerous, must have consisted for the most part of skilled workers of the type which formed the backbone of the parties in Philadelphia and New York.

There has been some disagreement among historians about how far workingmen influenced the course of national politics in the Jacksonian era. It has been maintained that Jackson owed much of his success to the support of urban labor voters. The whole question is somewhat artificial in view of the extent to which industry was still carried on in the countryside. But it is of course true that there were sections of the Jacksonian program—opposition to the banking system, for instance—which had a ready appeal to the artisans who had founded the workingmen's parties. Yet the very word "artisan" reminds us that there were many differences of status among the workingmen, and at a time when local issues were much more important in relation to national questions than they are now, it would be surprising if any generalizations about the political behavior of "labor" could readily be made. Statistical examination of the voting patterns of the poorer sections of the urban population have provided no very positive conclusions. It may tentatively be suggested that support for Jackson was strongest in the West and in the more rural sections of the eastern states; and that, with the exception of the active and vocal minority of artisans who ran the workingmen's parties, there was a strong tendency for the urban workers to divide on ethnic lines—the German and Irish immigrants supporting the Democratic party and the native Americans and British immigrants backing the Whigs. In this situation, both of the major parties found it worthwhile to bid for a larger share of the workers' votes: in the smaller towns they set out to "capture," and even to establish, "workingmen's parties" which might mobilize support for their candidates. And furthermore, they were willing to enact many of the workingmen's demands, such as educational reform and the abolition of imprisonment for debt—measures which both in New York and in Pennsylvania were passed shortly after the demise of the independent workingmen's parties.

Thus the major political parties still felt the pressure of the artisans' demands after their formal organizations had disappeared. There was always the danger, of course, that they might reappear. This was what in fact happened in the case of "Locofocoism" at New York. The former supporters of the workingmen's party in the city constituted an element inside Tammany, and some of their leaders had been sent to Albany as regular Democratic representatives; indeed, Ely Moore, the president of the New York General Trades Union, was elected to Congress—the first trade unionist to win this honor, although actually he was more of an opportunist politician than a man from the ranks of labor. But when in 1835 the workingmen found Tammany leaders supporting the chartering of new state banks, a rift occurred, and the workingmen decided to choose their own ticket of candidates for the next state elections. When an attempt was made to sabotage their meeting by turning off the gaslights, the workingmen managed to struggle through their agenda with the aid of candles lit by "locofoco" matches—hence the popular title of their party. The solidarity of the New York artisans at this time was strong, especially after a local judge in sentencing twenty journeymen tailors for conspiracy had argued, quite incorrectly, that the unions were "mainly upheld by foreigners." In 1838, the Tammany leaders finally came to terms with the "locofoco" group, accepting the substance of a declaration of rights which they drew up; and in 1840 the compact was cemented still more firmly by action on the national level—President Van Buren's executive order limiting the working day of federal employees to ten hours.

Meanwhile the middle 1830's saw a further development of trade unionism, particularly in the form of city federations of trades, which now existed not merely in the larger cities but also in many smaller centers in the West as well as on the Atlantic seaboard. This widespread activity led to contacts between various local societies in the same trades; the printers and shoemakers, as usual, led the way in holding national conventions of delegates of their craft. Furthermore, the New York General Trades Union sponsored a "National Trades Union" comprehending them all—the first attempt at a national organization of the trades ever to take place in the United States. In practice this did not amount to more than the summoning of an annual convention in New York City of delegates from city federations. The convention was held in three successive years, and delegates came from as far afield as Baltimore, Washington, and Cincinnati. Discussion centered on such topics as the need for union organization, the harmful effects of competition from convict labor, and the importance of securing the limitation of female employment. But in 1837, with the onset of a financial crisis and trade depression, the National Trades Union and the other national organizations, such as they were, all seem to have collapsed.

The panic of 1837 marks a breaking-point in the history of American labor. The fresh start of the 1840's was made in a new atmosphere. One important feature of the new period was the great increase in immigration, especially from Ireland, which rose to a peak after the potato famine toward the end of the decade. These Irishmen, mostly unskilled and ill-educated, crowded into the larger cities, especially Boston and New York, and rapidly squeezed the native American worker—including the free Negro—out of the humbler occupations such as domestic service and general labor. As time went on, they began to take a high proportion of the less skilled jobs in the factories of New England. The distinct tendency of wages in the factories to decline in the 1830's and 1840's, the westward movement of New England farmers, and the expansion of other occupations for women such as schoolteaching, led to the disappearance of that unique phenomenon, the cultured operative of the Lowell system. Her place was usually taken by the Irish immigrant, who was at first quite content with a low wage and poor conditions of work. With so many occupations falling to the foreign newcomer, whose habits of life seemed to the native American not merely strange but crude, it is not surprising that a general hostility to the immigrant grew up in those parts of the Union where they settled in large numbers.

This hostility took various forms, and varied considerably

in intensity, depending in part upon the degree of "foreignness" of the immigrants concerned. The English and Scots, being both Protestant and English-speaking, merged readily into the native population—a process rendered easier by the variety of skills which they brought with them. The Germans automatically encountered some prejudice owing to the language barrier and because some of them were Catholics; and, in New York at least, there were at first frequent complaints about their competition in the skilled trades. In the end, they came to be recruited into the trade societies of the city, either in separate German-speaking locals or mixed in with their English-speaking colleagues.

The unskilled Irishmen, almost invariably Catholics, and for the most part congregating in city slums, in spite of their knowledge of the English language proved the least assimilable at a time when anti-Catholic prejudice was strong in the United States. They were quite capable of maintaining prejudice and creating disturbances among themselves, as was shown as early as 1834 in the astonishing gang warfare among Irish laborers on the Chesapeake and Ohio Canal, which caused Andrew Jackson to send in the federal troops. But as time went on, religious rioting between Irish Catholics and native Americans became not uncommon in the larger cities; and in 1844 thirteen people were killed in disturbances of this character at Philadelphia. Later, the Mexican War and the rise of the slavery issue to a predominant position in national politics caused a diminution of anti-Catholic feeling; but the continued growth of immigration, combined with the disintegration of the Whig party, led to the emergence of the strongly nativist Know-Nothing movement in the early 1850's. In areas of heavy urban settlement by foreigners, such as New

England and the middle Atlantic states, Know-Nothing candidates secured striking electoral successes in the years 1852–56, although hardly anything of their policies of immigration restriction and limitation of voting rights was enacted.

It seems paradoxical at first sight that this period of labor history has been described as the era of "humanitarianism." Yet the title is not too difficult to explain. At a time when the workers themselves were divided by ethnic conflicts, when traditional crafts were being replaced or at least considerably disturbed by mechanical processes, and when the factory workers themselves largely consisted of women and children, it was difficult for a genuine labor movement to develop. Consequently, the way was open for middle-class reformers to air their views as to the best remedies for existing ills, and often to pass themselves off as the genuine representatives of labor. Fourier's utopian principles of social reorganization, for instance, were constantly propagated at workingmen's conferences by the assiduous Albert Brisbane, and owing to the support of Horace Greeley, the popular journalist, they secured considerable attention in the press. Self-supporting Fourierist or Owenite colonies were set up in suitably isolated places, but with little permanent success. These experiments did, however, encourage workingmen to take an interest in consumers' co-operation in the later 1840's. A number of "protective associations," as the co-operatives were called, came into existence for a brief period, only to disappear in most cases before many months had passed.

The most practical by far of the proposed solutions of labor's ills put forward at this time by middle-class reformers was the land-reform policy of George Henry Evans. Evans sought to rally the workers behind his National Reform Association with the object of securing a division of the national domain into homesteads for all. This program had a certain appeal to the urban workers, in view of the increasing difficulties which faced the poor man who wished to set himself up on a western homestead. But, of course, many families of comparatively limited resources were still managing to go west and acquire land; and so it proved difficult for Evans to persuade very many people that this issue ought to be the predominant one in national politics. All the same, as we shall see, his ideas were more successful in the end than were those of his fellow reformers.

All these reformers had the characteristic in common that they approached the problems of labor as it were from the outside. They were not themselves artisans, still less factory operatives, at the time that they were agitating for change. Rather they were zealous philanthropists, anxious to assist in solving the world's problems. Such generous enthusiasm was increasingly to be met in other spheres of activity; in fact, it was an indication of the increasing leisure available to those sections of the community which stood above the level of the manual worker. Abolitionism, the cause of women's rights, and the temperance movement were other directions in which the energies of the great American middle class came to be spent at this time.

The genuine labor movement of the 1840's was, as we have implied, feeble and ineffective. In the more prosperous years in the middle of the decade, a number of mechanics' and laborers' associations came into existence in New England. At Lowell there was even a Female Labor Reform Association, run by one of the factory girls, Sarah G. Bagley. These bodies were organized without distinctions of craft, and their prin-

37

cipal object was to reduce the hours of labor to something like the ten-hour standard that many of the artisans of New York and Philadelphia had secured in the 1820's or 1830's. In 1845 they held an Industrial Congress for the ventilation of their grievances, and other industrial congresses were held in subsequent years, some of them of national scope, some of them for individual states. The trouble was that these congresses all too often turned into factional disputes between the various middle-class reformers of the time.

Slowly, however, the skilled artisans began to organize their individual crafts on a local basis, to disentangle themselves from the reformers, and to overcome the ethnic rivalries which had weakened them for a decade. The Crimean War provided a breathing-space in which immigration temporarily declined, and generally prosperous conditions strengthened their position. Even the factory workers were able to win a reduction of their hours to eleven or ten; and the state legislatures were at long last willing to pass laws to the same end. Some of the craft societies once again began to contemplate the possibility of associating with societies of their own craft in other towns—an object that became all the more desirable as transportation facilities improved and the size of the market both for labor and for goods steadily enlarged. It had already been customary for local societies of the same craft to offer each other's members certain reciprocal privileges; now this could be systematized and the different locals could co-operate in fixing conditions of work and wages. In this way national unions came into existence, though naturally they were at first no more than weak federations of substantially autonomous local societies. The first to be formed was the National Typographical Union (1852), and this lead was followed by several other trades, of which the apparently successful ones were the Stone Cutters (1853), the Hat Finishers (1854), the Molders (1859) and the Machinists (1859). The building trades, having less need to establish uniformity of prices, were slower to establish links of this character. But in any case, the whole movement had made very little real progress before the outbreak of the Civil War.

Nothing has so far been said about developments in the South, where, as we saw in the last chapter, the institution of slavery and the plantation system made conditions radically different from those elsewhere in the Union. Jefferson and many other leaders of southern opinion late in the eighteenth century and early in the nineteenth had hoped that slavery, like indentured servitude, would prove unprofitable and so would move toward gradual extinction. But Eli Whitney's invention of the cotton gin in 1793, providing as it did a means of rapidly expanding the plantation system, gave a new lease of life to slavery. The slave trade was terminated in 1808, at which time the total number of Negro slaves amounted to more than a million; but natural increase, aided by a certain amount of illegal importation, raised the total to almost four million in 1860. There were, in addition, rather less than half a million free Negroes. In spite of the increase, the demand for slaves constantly pushed up their price, so that the deliberate breeding of Negro children became an important secondary consideration with the planters.

As the economic incentives to retain the institution became more apparent, hostility to slavery in the South gradually declined. As late as the 1820's there seemed to be as much support for abolition in the South as there was in the North, and there was much interest in the work of the Colonization Society, which sought, never with much success, to free the slaves and re-establish them upon the African continent. In the following decade, especially after the alarming and bloody rebellion led by the slave Nat Turner in Virginia in 1831, the southern attitude to slavery hardened; and the ensuing growth of abolitionist sentiment in the North only increased southern opposition to any change in the status quo. From the 1840's, the sectional conflict—which was at heart a conflict over the institution of slavery—increasingly dominated national politics; and the defense of slavery became the distinguishing feature of southern patriotism.

How did the slave fare in all this? Conditions varied so widely from one part of the South to another, from one type of employment to another, and especially from one master to another, that generalization is not easy; and as the whole question remains controversial, interpretations inevitably differ widely. The southern slaveholders, when challenged about their treatment of the slaves, pointed at once to the "wage slaves" of factory industry in the North, and argued that at least the Negro slaves did not suffer, as the factory workers did, from spells of unemployment or from loss of sustenance in sickness or old age. To this it could be replied that there were no known cases of fugitive "wage slaves" running away to the South, which they could have done with impunity, whereas there were plenty of Negroes who risked the perils and hardships of the underground railroad to escape to the North. The fact that the marriage of slaves had no legal status, and could be broken up by the will of the master, is in itself enough to show the whole world of difference between the position of the free man and the slave.

Social Experiments and Problem of Slavery

The most fortunate of the slaves, as a general rule, were those who had acquired certain skills of craftsmanship, for they were particularly valued and looked after and were often allowed to work on hire, retaining for their own advantage any of their earnings above a certain sum to which the master laid claim. Such men could sometimes put by their extra earnings to buy their freedom. Next to them, perhaps, were the domestic slaves on the large plantations, who lived with the master's family and shared some of their luxuries. Of the remainder of the plantation slaves, however, it is difficult to generalize, except to say that their lot was not likely to be a very happy one. On the large plantations, they were usually at the mercy of a paid white overseer, whose sole interest was to maintain the maximum crop production from the estate. His remedy for any infractions of discipline was the lash—a ready instrument of punishment sanctioned universally by the customs and law of the southern states. On the smaller plantations, the master himself would supervise the work of his slaves, and would often work by their side; but opinions differ as to whether, under such circumstances, the slaves were better off. Sometimes, no doubt, they would suffer from the sheer poverty or inefficiency of their masters.

The fact is that the institution of slavery was an evil thing, resulting in the degradation of all who operated under it, whether master or slave. But this must not blind us to certain important positive features of the life of the Negroes in America in this period. In spite of harsh conditions, they survived and multiplied to an extent that would have been impossible had they remained in Africa. Furthermore, they were able gradually to acquire something of the culture of their country —the language, if only rarely the arts of reading and writing;

and the Christian religion, on which they often put a different interpretation than that suggested by their masters. They were becoming "Americanized," as all immigrants had to be sooner or later, and this helped to equip them for the hardly less arduous life of the post-bellum era.

It was not to be expected that the small class of white industrial workers in the South, or the much larger class in the North, would sympathize very much with the grievances of the Negro. Unquestionably the competition of slave labor kept down the remuneration of free labor in the South: the wage of white textile workers in the southern states, for instance, was only two-thirds of what it was in the North. Yet at the same time the competition of large numbers of emancipated Negroes, able to move in search of jobs throughout the country, seemed to many white men to be an even more alarming possibility. The poor white southerner may have felt, consciously or subconsciously, that he needed the existence of slavery in order to assure himself of his status in the community; the northerner felt that he needed it in order to avoid a flood of competitors for jobs moving up from the South.

If under the existing state of things bitter conflict could arise between free Negroes and white workers in northern cities, what would happen after wholesale emancipation? In 1850 a widely circulated pamphlet by a workingman, H. F. Jones, under the title *Abolitionism Unveiled!* warned its readers that the "midas-eared Mammonites, self-styled Abolitionists" wished to bring southern Negroes into the North in order to "compete with and assist in reducing the wages of the white laborer." This sentiment was also expressed by Hermann Kriege, a leader of German-American labor—a group generally supposed to have been particularly strongly opposed to the maintenance of slavery. He declared that abolition "could not improve" the lot of the Negro, and would only serve to make "infinitely worse" the situation of white workers. Finally, whether or not they were afraid of the results of emancipation, the northern workers could not but be tempted to regard the cry of abolition as a red herring devised by the employing class to draw attention away from their own grievances. The fact that the most enthusiastic abolitionists were often persons of some substance in the community gave added weight to this impression.

In time, however, the attitude of northern labor to the question of emancipation began to alter. One reason for this was the intensity of the sectional conflict and of the propaganda to which it gave rise. Republican speakers and writers were not without subtlety in pointing out that any extension of slavery threatened the position of the free workingman. Another reason was the incorporation of a homestead plank in the program of the Republican party, which was at least partially along the lines of what Evans' National Reform Association had long been demanding. Abraham Lincoln himself, as a man of humble origin, had an important personal advantage in claiming the workingmen's votes. In addition, he showed real appreciation of the hopes and fears of northern labor when in 1860 he told an audience in New England:

I am glad to see that a system of labor prevails in New England under which laborers can strike when they want to. . . . I want every man to have the chance—and I believe a black man is entitled to it—in which he can better his condition—when he may look forward and hope to be a hired laborer this year and the next, work for himself afterward, and finally to hire men to work for him. . . . I desire that if you get too thick here, and find it hard to better your condition on this soil, you may have a chance to strike and go somewhere else, where you may not be degraded, nor have your family corrupted by forced rivalry with negro slaves.

In short, Lincoln proposed to the northern workers the solution of escape to the West and offered to barter this in return for their support against slavery. His party also sought the votes of the immigrants, by means of the so-called "Dutch plank," drafted by Carl Schurz, which guaranteed them against any limitation of their existing access to American citizenship. It was on this platform that both Lincoln and the Republicans were swept into power in the fateful elections of November, 1860—only to confront the secession of the southern states and the issue of civil war.

The special characteristics of American labor in colonial times, which were described in the last chapter, were hardly less marked in the greater part of the early national period. At first it seemed as if the heterogeneity of conditions would gradually diminish with the decline of servitude and with the gradual emergence of a coherent American nationality out of the welter of eighteenth-century immigrants. But after about 1830 two factors reversed this process—the growing consolidation of the institution of plantation slavery in the South and the enormous increase in immigration, especially from Ireland and Germany.

To these differences a further complication was added by the advance of industrial techniques. The development of the size of the market led in many trades to the growth of large-scale production and consequently to a decline in those industrial skills which had been painfully maintained or built up in the later colonial period. The introduction of power-driven machinery hastened these changes, particularly in textile manufacture. Thus the varieties of condition for American labor were increased, and the contrast between the factory industry of the North and middle Atlantic seaboard areas and the overwhelmingly rural occupations of the South and West became especially marked.

Yet the United States as a whole, not even excluding New England, remained a predominantly agricultural country. New York, which became in this period the largest American city, still had less than four hundred thousand inhabitants in 1845, although its rate of increase was rapid; and many of those engaged in industry either lived or had been brought up in the countryside. It might no longer be easy for a family without means or farming skills to secure access to the public domain, and to establish itself on a homestead in the West. All the same, even if all the western migrants were people with farming experience and accumulated savings, it is probably true, as Joseph Schafer has suggested, that many of them had contributed "a few years or seasons" to various industrial occupations. Their movement at least eased the position of those workers who stayed in the East and made them more able to cope with the fresh immigration from Europe. In this sense, the efficacy of the moving frontier as a "safety-valve" for labor in this period cannot be doubted.

American labor before the Civil War was closely linked with an agricultural, or at least rural, background. Up to 1860, as in the colonial era, most adult males had engaged for some part of their lives in the regular tasks of husbandry and the nurture of the crops. This was also true of most of the immigrants, and it must not be forgotten that many of them, especially those from Germany and Scandinavia, found their

American Labor

way almost directly to western homesteads, particularly in the plains bordering the Great Lakes. Thus although the industrial revolution had already profoundly affected the United States, the great bulk of the country's industrialization and urbanization was yet to come.

This rural background helped to preserve the marked social equality of American life that had come into existence before the Revolution. The Negro in the South, to be sure, remained an exception as before; and there may have been a certain tendency on the East Coast to look down upon the humbler, unskilled workers, who were often European immigrants used to a very low standard of life. But the reforms in public education, which made the schools of the Northeast the envy of European nations, were a guarantee that in succeeding generations these differences would disappear; and in the meantime the great bulk of the American population remained as equalitarian as they ever had been—in fact more so, insofar as they had so lately achieved almost universal white male suffrage.

Travelers from Europe still noticed the same contrasts with their own native lands—the independence and high wages of the manual worker, the relative uniformity of manners, the general diffusion of knowledge and intelligence. In the 1820's Mrs. Frances Trollope had noted the fact, regrettable to her, that servants could be hired only with difficulty, and that they expected to eat their meals with the family; in 1861 her son Anthony found that "the general level of material and intellectual well-being" was "infinitely higher in a new American than in an old European town." In the 1830's the most famous traveler of all, Alexis de Tocqueville, found numerous signs of the equalitarian tendencies of the country, and Harriet

Social Experiments and Problem of Slavery

Martineau, observing a demonstration by journeymen mechanics in New York, could hardly believe her eyes: "Surely never were such dandy mechanics seen; with sleek coats, glossy hats, gay watch-guards, and doeskin gloves!" Similar observations were not wanting a score of years later; and Richard Cobden, who revisited the United States in 1859 after an interval of twenty-four years, could conclude, "The people are far better off to my eye as compared with the Europe of today than they were in 1835 as compared with the old world at that time."

In spite of the vicissitudes of trade unionism, therefore, and the depressing effects of slavery and of heavy immigration, the conditions of American labor continued to impress the observant foreigner as uniquely favorable. However intractable the sectional issue might prove to be, this fact at least augured well for the future of the Republic.

Captains of Industry, Knights of Labor

The secession of the southern states in 1860–61 caused widespread temporary unemployment, owing to the dislocation of markets and the uncertainty of the future. But the demands of the armed forces soon made themselves felt, and from 1862 onward it was at least true of the industrial areas of the North that the war served to accentuate developments that were already taking place—the improvement of communications, the extended use of machinery, and the movement toward a factory economy. In those parts of the United States that were still controlled by the federal government—and they contained something like 85 per cent of the manufacturing capacity of the country—the cotton industry was the only major industry to suffer a serious setback, and this of course was due to the cutting-off of the source of raw materials. In the West, expansion continued apace, increasing the demand for agricultural machinery and for the building of railroads and their equipment. The industrial tariff system introduced by the Republican Congress gave the manufacturers a sense of confidence in the future and encouraged them to plan ahead. Great progress was made in the production of iron and steel, partly but by no means entirely to meet military requirements. The mass production of clothing and of boots and shoes was stimulated by the needs of the armies, but the principal technical change in both industries—the introduction of the sewing machine—had already begun a few years before the war. Production suffered little from the absence of men on military service. The new methods of manufacture depended less upon highly skilled workers than in the past, and it was not difficult to obtain fresh supplies of female and juvenile labor. Immigration continued during the war, and Congress in 1864 encouraged manufacturers to import craftsmen by legalizing contracts of service made abroad.

In the South, by contrast, a predominantly agrarian economy had to manage as best it could under conditions of blockade. Confederate manufacturers were content if they could produce makeshift substitutes for supplies formerly purchased from the North. The Confederate government itself had to assume direct responsibility for much of the production, owing to the lack of willing private contractors. Slave labor could of course be used as extensively as in peacetime, but the fear of slave revolts immobilized a substantial proportion of the available white manpower, and there was always a tendency for the plantation slaves to desert to the Federals when the battle-line came close to their homes. The fact that the war lasted altogether four years serves only to show that military success, in those days at least, depended on a great deal more than sheer economic superiority.

The expansion of northern industry proceeded with hardly

a pause at the end of the war, and its links with the West continued to develop rapidly. In 1869 the first transcontinental railroad was completed, but this marked no slowing down of railroad construction in general. The Middle West was drawn more and more into the manufacturing orbit. Iron ore from Lake Superior and coal from Illinois were shipped to furnaces in Pennsylvania, and as time went on new furnaces were built closer to the sources of supply, notably at Chicago. With the introduction of the Bessemer process, steel began to take the place of iron for most structural purposes; and by the 1880's the American output of Bessemer steel was rivaling that of Britain.

Along with the expansion of the market and the sheer growth of industry, there went a constantly increasing mastery of manufacturing techniques. In many industries we can perceive constant infringements of the position of the skilled craftsman, arising from the introduction of machinery (as in clothing and boots and shoes) or from changes in the market and in the scale of manufacture (as in iron-molding or in cigar-making). It is true that some skills were developing as a consequence—notably that of the machinist, whose task it was to make the machinery that broke down other crafts. But the general picture was one of much unrest among the trades and much concern about the introduction of "green hands" or unskilled labor to do jobs that were formerly the preserve of the skilled. According to a visiting English craftsman, apprenticeship had broken down so far that journeymen were being turned out "as if by steam." This process was of course facilitated by the high postwar rates of immigration, whether skilled or unskilled.

There were other grievances, too, which affected labor as

a whole and not just the skilled. During the war there was a steep inflation of prices, which for some time left wages far behind. The prewar level of real wages was not restored for a decade. The worst sufferers were the women and children, especially in the clothing industry: it was not easy for them to bargain for wage increases. In the novel circumstances of wartime, the sufferings of the poorer sections of the community were not sufficiently recognized. Labor in general had cause to complain of the provisions of the 1863 draft law, which discriminated in favor of the wealthy by allowing exemption on pain of a $300 fine. The enforcement of this law caused rioting in New York, particularly among Irish immigrants. In other parts of the country, strikes affecting war production were prohibited by military order and broken if necessary by the use of troops. These at least were only temporary discontents; but there were plenty of other causes of unrest which remained after the war was over. One of them was the competition in certain trades of convict labor, which was to remain as an irritant to many trades for long years to come. Another was the "store-order" method of payment of wages, by which workers were forced to buy goods from company stores. This was a feature of the large-scale industry which had already begun to develop before the war. Even the Homestead Act of 1862, which had been the Republican party's principal concession to the labor interest, provided little relief, except perhaps for Civil War veterans. For the poorer workers, its provisions were largely nullified by the existence of pre-emption arrangements and by generous grants of good land to railroads and other corporations.

But if the 1860's form a period of labor unrest, this was as nothing to the distress occasioned by the prolonged depression of 1873–79. A financial panic in 1873 was followed by several years of industrial slump, in which production of manufactures fell by about a third. Unemployment was widespread: in 1873–74 it was calculated that in New York City a quarter of the total labor force was out of work. These urban workers in most cases no longer had the resort of the early New England factory girls in bad times—return to the countryside. There was consequently a severe strain on the charity societies, and special conferences were held to discuss the co-ordination of their efforts. No other depression in American history, except that of the 1930's, was so severe in its immediate effects or so lasting in its consequences.

Meanwhile the South was making a painful recovery from the effects of war. The plantation economy was disrupted by the end of slavery, and in its place there developed a system, not of wage-labor, for the planters did not have the liquid resources for this, but of sharecropping. The sharecroppers were poor whites or Negroes; they pledged a large share of their crops in advance to planters, or to merchants and bankers who had the ready cash to buy the planters out. In return for this, they received tenancies and credit at local stores—the stores themselves usually being owned by the same planters or merchants. Few Negro farmers could escape from this relationship, which was virtually one of servitude—not a great advance, in fact, upon the earlier system of slavery, although the Negroes did at last obtain some basis for continuous family life. Industrialization made little progress in the South; it took several years to replace the devastation of the final war years, and when that had been done, there was a limited expansion of cotton manufacture and also of mining in some areas. But in general, the economic position of the

Negro remained very difficult, and his political gains from emancipation and from the reconstruction period were steadily lost as the rule of the southern white aristocracy was reasserted. His only hope, it might seem, would have been to move north to seek employment in the more prosperous industrial areas. But as we shall see, this avenue of escape was, to say the least, precarious.

Although the early dislocation of trade and the unemployment of the first year of the Civil War caused a temporary collapse of labor-union organization, it soon began to revive. The return to full employment to meet military needs and the rapid rise in prices which followed led to a resumption of activity by the trade societies, at least in northern industrial areas. Once again, the great bulk of this activity took the form of the foundation of local unions of particular trades, and their combination into city federations or "trades' assemblies," as they were called. In 1864, while the war was still continuing, an attempt was made to unite the trades' assemblies into an "International Industrial Assembly of North America." The title "International" was used to indicate that some of the trades' assemblies which it was hoped to include were in Canada. But the inaugural convention at Louisville, Kentucky, was a fiasco: only twelve delegates appeared, and no further meeting was held.

Much more significant for the future was the revival of the national unions, several of which had been founded in the late 1850's. The constant extension of the market for most industrial products and the ease with which labor could now migrate from region to region made national organization imperative if the unions were to be effective. The new development was not only general—there were ten national unions founded within two years at the end of the war—but it was also very soundly based in several industries.

The iron-molders, for instance, under the powerful leadership of William Sylvis of Philadelphia, eliminated much of the autonomy of the locals, including the right to strike without national permission, and built up a central strike fund based upon compulsory contributions. At its peak in the 1860's, a majority of skilled workers in the trade belonged to this union, and it was able to secure both a high rate of wages and an effective control of apprenticeship. For the first time, it seemed, organized labor had come to have real influence upon industrial wage-rates and working-conditions in at least one trade. But Sylvis' success did not last long: a national combination of employers, together with the depression of 1867, forced wages down again and led to a rapid loss of union membership; and by 1868 Sylvis, shaken by his experience and worried about the constant introduction of less skilled workers into the foundries, began to despair of craft unionism and to shift his attention to the prospects of producers' co-operation. He persuaded his union to establish a co-operative foundry which, however, soon collapsed owing to lack of capital.

A roughly similar cycle of events took place in the boot and shoe trade, although here there was no leader of the stature of Sylvis, and the union at its peak was never quite so successful. In 1867 a society for boot and shoe workers came into existence under the title of "Knights of St. Crispin." As the title indicates, there was at this time a certain tendency to copy the forms of the masonic orders when founding trade unions. The Crispins grew rapidly and by April, 1871, had a total of 327 lodges. Its early strikes usually proved successful, and its peak membership, scattered widely across the United States, may have been as large as fifty thousand. But even this total did not constitute as high a proportion of the workers in the trade as the molders had; and the rapid transformation of the industry caused by the introduction of machinery suitable for unskilled labor was the undoing of the Crispins. By the early 1870's its leaders and several of the lodges were trying to found co-operatives, with little success; and the whole body was soon in a state of collapse, reviving only faintly in 1875–78.

Although both these unions had somewhat checkered careers, the molders were at least able to stay in existence as a national union; and other national unions were able to do likewise. Several new ones had come into existence in the late 1860's or early 1870's and proved able to survive the later depression years. One of them was the Machinists and Blacksmiths, which represented a craft rapidly developing out of the industrial revolution. Its secretary, Jonathan Fincher, ran the outstanding labor newspaper of the period, *Fincher's Trades Review,* and the national union expanded to some eighteen thousand members by 1873. At this date the Bricklayers and the International Typographical Union, both still highly decentralized in form, could probably claim about equal numbers. The largest union of the period, however, was that of the anthracite miners, who were concentrated in eastern Pennsylvania. Organized by John Siney in 1868, they formed a Workingmen's Benevolent Association which, like the British mining unions on which it was patterned, secured an agreement for the payment of wages on a sliding scale in accordance with the price of coal. Siney also succeeded in organizing the bituminous miners, but only for a very brief period. Even his anthracite union succumbed in the 1870's to the pressure of bad times, the increasing concentration of owner- ship in the industry, and the skilful use of recent immigrants as strikebreakers.

The national unions played a prominent role in the estab- lishment of a national organization of labor after the Civil War. The body that they helped to sponsor, the National Labor Union, was founded in 1866 at a convention at Balti- more; and the following year it adopted a constitution drawn up by William Sylvis. But the national unions were not yet a dominant element in the labor movement as a whole, and the bulk of the delegates at the conventions of the National Labor Union were drawn from local trades' assemblies or from local associations formed to agitate for the eight-hour day—the new labor demand pioneered by the machinist Ira Steward of Boston. Even the leaders of the national unions, as we have seen, became very unsure of their industrial future at times. Sylvis, indeed, not only took up the idea of pro- ducers' co-operation but also interested himself in national political action. He believed that labor needed to mobilize every ally in order to escape from its difficulties, and that it should collaborate with the Negroes, with the movement for women's emancipation, and even with the workers of Europe. He also advocated Edward Kellogg's monetary theories and put forward a cheap money policy based upon the greenback notes introduced during the Civil War. "When a just monetary system has been established," he wrote, "there will no longer exist a necessity for trade unions."

Sylvis died suddenly in 1869 at the early age of forty-one; and after his death the National Labor Union soon disintegrated. The remaining national union leaders were opposed to its concentration upon political activity, and in 1870 they withdrew, with the sole exception of the Crispins. They were replaced by middle-class reformers, many of whom had personal political ambitions. In 1872 the National Labor Union met to choose a ticket for the presidential election, but its candidate for the presidency, Judge David Davis of Illinois, was only interested in obtaining the Democratic party nomination, and he withdrew when he failed to get this. This fiasco virtually sealed the fate of the National Labor Union.

The National Labor Union may seem to have been a total failure, marking no advance upon earlier national organizations. There were, however, some novel features to be credited to it. One of its leaders, Richard Trevellick of the Ships' Carpenters and Caulkers International Union, had been established in Washington in 1868 to lobby for the eight-hour day, and he was influential in securing the passage of an Act of Congress to limit the hours of federal employees to eight. It was not easy to secure observance of the Act, but its enactment was nevertheless an advance.

The National Labor Union was also the first body representing American labor to establish links with European labor movements. In 1869, A. C. Cameron of Chicago was sent as a delegate to a meeting of the First International at Basel in Switzerland. One object of his trip was to establish some means whereby the American unions might supervise the migration to America of European workers belonging to their particular crafts. The ironworkers in particular had suffered by the import of laborers under contract, especially from Britain. It did not prove possible, however, to establish any machinery to deal with this problem, perhaps partly because the interests of the European unions ran counter to those of the American unions. Finally, the National Labor Union, at least while it was under Sylvis' leadership, endeavored to give a positive lead to its constituent bodies on the subject of Negro unionism.

The situation of Negro industrial labor at this time was most unenviable. Northern white workers' fears of Negro competition had led to occasional violence even during the Civil War, for instance among the Cincinnati steamboat hands in 1862 and in the draft riots at New York in 1863. Many unions did not allow Negroes to join their ranks, and when the National Labor Union discussed the question at its congresses in 1867 and 1868, it could reach no agreement. Finally, with the encouragement of Sylvis, nine Negro delegates were seated at the 1869 congress, and a resolution was accepted that the organization "knows no North, no South, no East, no West, neither color nor sex. . . ." It was another matter, however, to persuade the national unions, or more particularly the locals, to accept Negro membership. Discrimination continued, and for several years Frederick Douglass' son, Lewis H. Douglass, was kept out of the Columbia (Washington, D.C.) local of the National Typographical Union. Negro leaders gradually realized that they would be obliged to organize on their own; and in December, 1869, a Colored National Labor Union came into temporary existence at Washington, D.C., with various objects including the establishment of an employment agency for skilled Negro workers and the encouragement of co-operatives as a guarantee against discrimination. The Negro leaders, who were staunch Republicans, finally withdrew from the National Labor Union when it went in for independent politics.

Captains of Industry, Knights of Labor

No sooner was the National Labor Union dead than the national trade unions attempted to set up a fresh organization more to their liking. In a circular summoning a convention in 1873, they emphasized that they would do all in their power to prevent their new brainchild from "deteriorating" into a political party; and they announced that they had "no Agrarian ideas; we neither believe or preach the doctrine that Capital is robbery." Their interest was limited to such strictly practical aims as legislation to protect trade unions, the establishment of the eight-hour day, and the abolition of contract labor immigration. When the convention met, the majority of delegates represented national unions. All the same, after a heated debate they did decide to support the greenback policy of financial reform, which was the political issue of the day. Independent political action, however, was disavowed.

It may be that this Industrial Congress—or Industrial Brotherhood, as it was called from 1874—would have established itself as a permanent body, given a background of normal industrial conditions in the country as a whole. But its foundation coincided with the beginning of the depression; and as a result the national unions, faced with heavy calls on their limited resources, rapidly lost interest in the Industrial Brotherhood and let it die. Once again—and for the last time—there was a period in which no organization existed with a reasonable claim to represent the labor movement as a whole.

The field was thus left open, as it had been in the 1840's, for a variety of individuals, many of them never having been employed in industry, to claim to represent the labor interest. Some of them were currency reformers whose focus of activity was the Greenback party, which they expected the workingmen to support. The Greenback party was in fact largely financed by its presidential candidate for the 1876 election, the veteran manufacturer Peter Cooper; and the bulk of his support in the election, which totaled but a hundred thousand votes, came from the rural districts of the West. Another body of the time which claimed the interest of the workers was the Order of the Sovereigns of Industry, which was an industrial counterpart of the farmers' National Grange: its aim was to establish co-operatives, and at its peak in 1875 it may have had a membership of about forty thousand, mostly in New England. Its members operated a number of co-operative stores on the English "Rochdale" pattern, but it had no success with co-operative production. The industrial depression, combined with poor management of many of the stores, led to its collapse in 1878.

By this time the condition of most of the industrial workers throughout the country was very difficult. The national trade unions had suffered heavy losses of membership, and, of about thirty which were in existence early in the 1870's, only eight or nine now survived. The collapse of the miners' unions resulted in a state approaching anarchy in some of the mining districts, and a series of murders led to secret investigations on behalf of the employers by a private detective agency, the Pinkertons. In 1875–76, on the basis of evidence secured by a Pinkerton detective, a number of Irishmen were tried on charges of murder and conspiracy in a secret society called the "Molly Maguires." No less than ten of them were executed, although the evidence against them does not now seem very convincing.

Elsewhere, too, severe economic distress and the absence of unions led to violence. On the Baltimore and Ohio Railroad, wage cuts in 1877 resulted in spontaneous strikes and rioting which was halted only by the intervention of federal troops. Worse still, similar economies on the Pennsylvania Railroad precipitated strikes and rioting which culminated in the deaths of twenty-six members of a mob in Pittsburgh; and this was followed by three days of continued rioting and looting in the city, with damage to property estimated at five million dollars. Of course, the extent of these disasters was largely due to the incompetence of the law enforcement authorities. But they shocked the whole country and stimulated the growth of a sense of class solidarity among the American workers. The divergence between the interests of employer and worker and the increasing loss of personal contact between the two sides of industry as the scale of manufacturing increased were helping to develop class feeling in the United States; but the great strikes of 1877 acted as a catalyst in making people consciously aware of social distinctions.

We can trace four different effects of these events. One of them was a sudden increase of labor interest in politics, resulting in the formation once more of local workingmen's parties; another was the emergence of an agitation against foreign, and particularly Chinese, immigration; and a third was the development of Marxian Socialism. A fourth result, which must be treated separately, was the growth of interest in a Pennsylvania secret society, the Knights of Labor.

As we have seen, in 1876 the Greenback party had been almost entirely lacking in labor support. But in the fall of 1877 the workingmen returned to politics in large numbers, holding meetings of their own and forming local organizations, but also pressing for an alliance with the Greenback party. The result was a convention of "labor and currency reformers" at Toledo in February, 1878. This meeting comprised a number of farmers and businessmen as well as labor leaders, but there could be no doubt this time about the strength of labor enthusiasm. The climax of the movement came in the congressional elections of 1878, when the total Greenback vote amounted to over a million, and fourteen representatives were elected to Congress. The party fell to pieces soon after the elections, however, partly owing to the withdrawal of the existing greenback currency on January 1, 1879, and partly owing to the gradual revival of trade in the course of the following year.

The anti-Chinese agitation, which centered in California where nearly all the Chinese were, could be ascribed in general to the depression which occasioned a great deal of unemployment in San Francisco and elsewhere. It was significant, however, that the anti-Chinese riots took place directly after news of the trouble on the railroads in 1877. Chinatown in San Francisco was attacked by a mob, and there was much damage to property there; and shortly afterward an Irish immigrant, Dennis Kearney, organized the "Workingmen's Party of California" on a platform of Chinese exclusion. This party, run by Kearney in despotic fashion and with a violence of language that constantly threatened fresh violence, was successful in the 1878 elections in winning a large proportion of seats at a state constitutional convention. In 1879 it elected many members of the state legislature and also a mayor of San Francisco. The party went to pieces in 1880–81; but by this time the issue had grown to national importance, and in 1882 Congress voted to prohibit Chinese immigration altogether for a period of twenty years.

Meanwhile a Socialist movement had been developing, principally in New York City and Chicago. The growing strength

of Socialism in Germany and in the Hapsburg Empire is enough
to account for its success among German-speaking immigrants;
its gradual progress beyond their ranks owed something to the
new American environment. The Socialists had a good deal
of influence in a German trades' assembly which existed in
New York and also in the national unions of German workers,
the Furniture Workers, and the German-American Typo-
graphia, both of which were organized in 1873. Various local
groups and factions of Socialists were united in 1876 into the
Workingmen's party of the United States, which at the end
of 1877 became known as the Socialist Labor Party. Its members in 1878–79 ran a short-lived International Labor Union,
which had several thousand members among the textile operatives at Fall River and Paterson. This was a gallant but unsuccessful attempt to organize the unskilled workers along with
the skilled. In Chicago the Socialists picked up some English-
speaking support, gained influence on the Chicago Trades
Council, and by 1879 had elected four aldermen to the City
Council. The early 1880's, however, saw strife among the Socialists as a result of the emergence of an Anarchist faction,
which developed under the influence of the most recent immigrants from Germany and Austria. In spite of this, Socialism
was already a force to be reckoned with inside the American
labor movement.

The Order of the Knights of Labor originated before the
depression of the 1870's, but it was to the depression that the
organization owed its sudden development on the national
scene. The Order was founded by some members of a collaps-
ing garment cutters' benefit society at Philadelphia, the most
active of whom, Uriah Stephens, had originally been trained

for the ministry. Stephens, who was a Mason and who had some knowledge of Greek, was able to provide the Order with much of its ritual. The locals of the Order were called "local assemblies," and a minimum of five local assemblies could be grouped together as a "district assembly." Eventually a "general assembly" came into existence, which elected officers and a general executive board to supervise the Order. The local and district assemblies already had officers, some of whom were purely social or ritualistic in function. In each assembly the principal executive officer was called the "Master Workman."

The Order gradually won members in the trades in the Philadelphia area, and by 1873 it had more than eighty local assemblies, all of them apparently confined to particular trades. Thereafter, however, it spread more rapidly, taking advantage of the collapse of the unions in the depression. The fact that it was a secret organization was a real advantage at a time when union members could easily be victimized. Soon it had assemblies in West Virginia, Ohio, Indiana, and Illinois, as well as in Pennsylvania. Many of these assemblies consisted solely of members of one particular trade, but some of them were "mixed assemblies," that is to say, they consisted of workers from a variety of trades or no trade at all. Although Stephens, as District Master Workman of District Assembly No. 1, had a certain seniority of position in the Order, its development began to get out of hand as rival districts chartered fresh locals with identical numbers. By the middle 1870's, there was an obvious need for a central authority.

Accordingly, a constitution was adopted at a general convention in 1878. Stephens was elected Grand Master Workman, and a secretary-treasurer and a general executive board of five members were also chosen. The preamble and platform of the deceased Industrial Brotherhood were taken over almost verbatim, including its recommendation of co-operative enterprises and other old nostrums such as homesteads, a workman's lien law, and the abolition of prison labor competition. One really important innovation was the introduction of a per capita tax on all members which was to be paid to the general executive.

By this time the secrecy of the Order had ceased to be an advantage. After the episode of the "Molly Maguires" people were apt to think of a secret labor society as being necessarily criminal. The Catholic Church also disapproved of secret societies and disliked certain quasi-religious elements in its ritual. At a meeting of the General Assembly in 1879 the Order went some way to meeting these objections, allowing local or district assemblies to emerge somewhat into the open. Stephens, however, who was a Protestant, disapproved of these concessions, and resigned from the leadership, being replaced as Grand Master Workman by Terence V. Powderly, a Catholic born of immigrant Irish parents. In 1881 Powderly persuaded the Order to remove the quasi-religious element from the ritual and also to abandon much of its remaining secrecy. But the difficulty with the Church was not yet over. In 1884 Cardinal Taschereau of Quebec, after consultations with the Holy See, issued a condemnation of the Knights; and it was not until a further three years had elapsed that Cardinal Gibbons of Baltimore, who favored recognition of the Order, was able to secure Vatican approval. By that time it was too late for the Catholic support to have any distinctive influence on the future of the Order.

After the abandonment of much of its secrecy in 1881, however, the Order expanded rapidly. The per capita payments of tax to the general executive indicate that the membership rose from 19,000 in 1881 to 111,000 in 1885. This growth was accompanied by important internal changes. A high proportion of the new members were recruited in the West, on the industrial frontier where skills were breaking down and workers were inclined to move rapidly from job to job—rural or urban, industrial or commercial. Many of the new recruits to the Knights were in fact farmers, others were small shopkeepers and the like. They resented the influence of the organized artisans in the movement, and as members of mixed assemblies they formed a counterpoise to the trade assemblies, which previously had been predominant. They favored political action in conjunction with the farmers' organizations in order to defeat the growing monopoly power of the banks and the railroads: but they regarded the national trade unions as incipient monopolies also, and disliked having their contributions used for the furtherance of strictly trade objects.

Yet the Order had grown up in the East, and some of its trade assemblies were really national unions in all but name. The most remarkable example of all was the Window Glass Workers, which appeared in the hierarchy of the Order in the humble guise of "Local Assembly 300." This body, after winning a five months' strike in 1883–84 with financial support from the general executive, was in virtually complete control of the entire window-glass labor force in the United States. It obtained a tight grip on the proportion of apprentices in the trade, and its only weakness was that it could not control the immigration of skilled workers from Europe. In 1884, however, it embarked upon two courses of action designed to eliminate even this difficulty. It sent organizers to all the centers of the window-glass trade in Europe, in order to unionize the entire world trade; and with the aid of the leadership of the Order it applied vigorous pressure at Washington in order to secure congressional legislation prohibiting the import of labor on contract. In both these enterprises, ambitious as they were, Local Assembly 300 came very close to success: it established the Order among the glass workers of Britain and Belgium, from whom it spread to a variety of trades, but it did not quite win control of the European window-glass industry; it secured the passing of the Foran Act in 1885, which provided penalties against those who imported contract labor, but the Act made no provision for the appointment of inspectors to see that this was enforced. The Foran Act, though frequently amended in later years, was always easily evaded, and its effect was negligible.

The Window Glass Workers of America were a very small body of workers, probably not amounting to more than about fifteen hundred; and their story is relevant here only insofar as it shows how the interests of an exclusive craft could sometimes be served by association with the Knights. The universal appeal of the Order was undoubtedly of assistance to the craft union in its organizing in Europe, and it was of especial advantage when lobbying at Washington to be able to pose as the entire American working class. At the same time, the Order's leaders benefited by having the Window Glass Workers in affiliation, and in times of financial difficulty they could borrow money from the usually ample treasury of Local Assembly 300.

From what has been said, it will be seen that there were a number of different interests inside the Order, not readily reconcilable at all times. Nor was Powderly a sufficiently powerful personality to impose a degree of consistency upon the Order's policies, as Sylvis had done with the National Labor Union and Gompers was to do with the American Federation of Labor. A scholarly-looking man of indifferent physique, he was a good speaker but a poor administrator. Sensitive and vain, he saw his problems as leader of the Order in largely personal terms, and in the process of remaining as Grand Master Workman (which he did until 1893) he gradually sacrificed the position of control which he had originally won.

Powderly had, however, done much to shape the development of the Order in the early 1880's, not only by removing much of its secrecy and helping to win it the approval of the Catholic Church, but also by making the boycott, rather than the strike, its most favored weapon against recalcitrant employers. It was not for nothing that he was a vice-president of the Irish Land League. But it was his misfortune that the boycott was not universally valuable in all trades; and although he disapproved of strikes, he frequently found the Order involved in them, was forced to intervene in person, and got the blame whenever they failed. In the crisis of the Order in 1885–86, Powderly was sorely tried but found sadly wanting. But to understand the complexity of the situation with which he was faced, it is necessary to say something of other developments in American trade unionism in the early 1880's.

From 1879, with the return of better trade conditions, the national unions began to revive. In the following years new unions were founded, old ones re-established, and the membership grew apace. In 1881 their leaders began to think of combining to form a national federation along the lines of the British Trades Union Congress, which would lobby at Washington after the fashion of the T.U.C. Parliamentary Committee. Although they were not initially hostile to the Knights of Labor, they did not regard the Order as a suitable intermediary for this purpose, in view of the characteristics which it had developed of secrecy, at least up to 1881, of centralization, at any rate in theory, and of willingness to adopt the "mixed" form of organization, which ran counter to the interests of the trades.

Accordingly, the national unions held a convention of their own at Pittsburgh in November, 1881, and established a body which they called "The Federation of Organized Trades and Labor Unions of the United States and Canada." It was decided that representation at future conventions, which were to be annual, would be weighted in favor of the larger national unions; and a small legislative committee of five was appointed with a secretary (W. H. Foster of the Cincinnati Trades Assembly) but no president. A platform was adopted which contained numerous labor demands of the traditional type, but which omitted co-operation and emphasized instead the need for federal and state legislation to protect trade-union property, such as had lately been adopted in Britain.

The growth of the Federation was at first slow. It was hindered by the recurrence of bad times in 1884–85, which were, to be sure, not as prolonged as in the 1870's but which caused a setback to the national unions. In 1884 a number of strikes initiated by unions were defeated: the Fall River Cotton Spinners were broken by the introduction of Swedish strikebreakers, and the Ohio Miners were defeated after six months in the same way, armed Pinkertons being used to protect a mixed body of Swedes, Italians, Poles, and Hungarians, who had been recruited from the labor bureaus in the big cities.

The Knights of Labor, on the other hand, were conspicuously successful with Powderly's favorite weapon, the boycott, which could be used very effectively against stores, saloons, and suppliers of food, drink, and clothing. The power of all the workers as consumers was thus mobilized to support a section of them as producers. Of the national unions independent of the Knights, only the Typographers and the Cigar Makers could benefit readily from a boycott, and the Cigar Makers preferred the more positive pressure of the "union label" to encourage people to buy union-made goods.

The following year, 1885, was a year of rapid growth for both the unions and the Knights—a fact which was to lead them into serious conflict. The Knights, profiting by their success with the boycott and with the Foran Act (passed in February, 1885) were already expanding rapidly. In the spring of 1885 they seemed to have real success at last with strike action. Members of the Order working three lines of the Gould railroad system—the Missouri Pacific, the Missouri Kansas and Texas, and the Wabash—launched an unpremeditated strike against wage reductions, and Gould, taken by surprise, at once gave way. A second strike on the Wabash line in the summer resulted in a settlement negotiated with the management by Powderly and his colleagues of the general executive—an event that gave them a rather undeserved prestige. In addition to all this, the Knights benefited from a revival of interest in the eight-hour day agitation. As a result, membership in the Order suddenly mushroomed from 111,000 in July, 1885, to well over 700,000 a year later. The national unions were also increasing in size, though not quite so spectacularly. The Federation of Organized Trades had carried a resolution in 1884 optimistically setting May 1, 1886, as the day for the inauguration of an eight-hour system in all trades. Partly as a consequence, but also because of the generally improving economic situation, the membership of the unions was rising. Agitation thus grew in the early months of 1886 as the workers looked forward to universal strike action for the eight-hour day.

Faced with this prospect Powderly, as was to be expected, pursued a rather timid course. In March he issued a secret circular to the assemblies to say that he was not prepared to authorize strikes on May 1. This did not prevent the assemblies, and still less the unions, from taking action as they had intended. It was calculated at the time that some 340,000 workers took part in the movement: of these, no less than 150,000 secured shorter hours without striking, and 190,000 actually had to quit their jobs when the day came. Forty-two thousand of the strikers also secured concessions from their employers. The center of the strike was Chicago, where altogether 80,000 took part.

The whole movement, however, which looked as if it would be an unqualified success, was damaged by unexpected events on May 4. A meeting in Haymarket Square, Chicago, was being addressed by some of the local Anarchist leaders when police advanced to break it up. At this point a bomb was thrown at the police, killing one officer and wounding others. The incident caused an immediate revulsion of feeling against all protest movements and undoubtedly damaged the Knights. In spite of the absence of conclusive evidence of their guilt, seven Anarchist leaders, all of them German-speaking except one, were condemned to death; of these, two were reprieved, one committed suicide in prison, and four were actually hanged. The one English-speaking member of the group, Albert Parsons, who was one of those hanged, was also a member of the Knights of Labor. Powderly took care to dissociate the Order from the outrage and also from all links with Anarchism, but he could not entirely separate them in the public mind. Also on May 4, the Knights suffered a severe industrial defeat in the collapse of a fresh strike on the Gould railroad network. On this occasion the strikers were forced to return to work without any sort of agreement, and many of them were charged with illegal acts against the companies in the course of the strike and suffered various penalties as a result. Membership of the Knights on the southwestern railroads was virtually eliminated.

Then, in October of the same year, the Chicago meatpacking employers, who had conceded the eight-hour day to their workers, withdrew the concession on the ground that it was not universal in the trade. The workers at once went on strike, but Powderly, convinced that it was a losing battle, in November sent a telegram instructing them to give way on pain of expulsion from the Order. Although this may have been the best course, it made Powderly highly unpopular in Chicago and severely damaged the prestige of the Knights. Of course, Powderly's position was a difficult one, for he had no control over the initiation of strikes by local or district assemblies, but was responsible for declaring whether or not they should be supported by the Order as a whole. But in this particular situation he was to blame for not taking the trouble to visit Chicago to see the situation for himself. It did not occur to him that a strike on a defensive issue was often a good opportunity for "organizing the unorganized," which in turn would lead to victory.

Meanwhile the Federation of Organized Trades and the

other national unions which did not yet belong to either the Federation or the Knights were beginning to feel the competition of the assemblies of the Order. The Cigar Makers, in particular, had suffered an internal schism which led a large section of their New York membership to form a local assembly of the Knights. This local joined District Assembly 49—a large and influential body led by a group of German Socialists, sometimes known as the "Home Club," who were on principle hostile to the pretensions of the craft unions.

To deal with this situation, a number of the leaders of the trade unions got together to summon a special meeting which would, they hoped, launch an association more comprehensive than the Federation of Organized Trades had been. The special meeting, which was called for May 13, 1886, in Philadelphia, was sponsored by W. H. Foster, the secretary of the Federation of Organized Trades, and by several officials of the national unions, including Adolph Strasser of the Cigar Makers. The meeting, they declared, was "to protect our respective organizations from the malicious work of an element who openly boast that trade unions must be destroyed." Its outcome was in fact a draft "treaty" or rather list of demands which was presented to the general executive of the Knights. According to this, the Knights were to disband their trade assemblies in the trades organized by the national unions and were to refrain from recruiting in those trades unless they had the sanction of the unions. There were also to be strict regulations against any intervention by the Knights in strikes involving union members.

It is possible that the Knights might have persuaded the union leaders to regard this "treaty" as merely a basis for negotiations. There were probably at least some on both sides who would have welcomed an opportunity to come to terms. But in each camp there was also a powerful element hostile to any compromise: in the unions, it was the leadership of the Cigar Makers, notably Adolph Strasser and Samuel Gompers; in the Order, it was the "Home Club." As a result, for some time the Knights did nothing about the proposed "treaty," and the trade unions went ahead to call a convention to establish a "Trades Congress," which would actively promote the formation of trade unions and local trades' councils. This meeting was held at Columbus, Ohio, in December, 1886. From its deliberations emerged the "American Federation of Labor," and the Federation of Organized Trades was absorbed into this new body.

While the inaugural meeting of the American Federation of Labor was going on, the general executive of the Knights at last bestirred itself to the extent of sending a committee to negotiate. Agreement by now was unlikely, for District Assembly 49 had effected an alliance with the western agrarian element in the Order at the expense of what trade sentiment there was, and consequently it dominated the general executive. The executive board of the Knights, therefore, ignored the "treaty" and merely put forward as a counterproposal an exchange of working cards between the Order and the unions. The latter could not possibly accept this, in view of their exclusive attitude to trade questions; and as neither side would proceed further, the negotiations fell through. The convention of the American Federation of Labor condemned the Knights for supporting the rebel Cigar Makers, and shortly afterward the general executive of the Knights officially confirmed a decision by District 49 that its members had to leave the International Union of Cigar Makers on pain of expulsion from the Order. The confirmation was later withdrawn, but by that time the damage had been done; the two national centers of the labor movement were already engaged in hostilities.

At first, it seemed as if the Knights might prove victorious. Efforts were made, not entirely without success, to recruit trade unions into the Order as national trade assemblies. But District Assembly 49 and the other mixed assemblies opposed concessions to local trade assemblies already organized inside the Order, which wished to establish themselves on a national basis; and this led to a gradual loss of trade assemblies. The Boot and Shoe Workers Union and the National Association of Machinists were both founded in 1889 as a result of secessions from the Order. The Miners, who had learned to respect the value of secrecy, and the Brewery Workers, who benefited substantially by the boycott, were among the last to leave. Gradually the membership of the Order declined—to 250,000 by the summer of 1887, to 100,000 in 1890, to 75,000 in 1893. In 1893 Powderly was replaced as General Master Workman, as a result of another combination between the Socialists of District Assembly 49 and the western agrarian element. His place was taken by James R. Sovereign, the editor of a farmers' paper in Iowa, who favored a policy of political action in conjunction with the farmers' organizations. But Sovereign thereupon quarreled with the Socialists, who then withdrew from the Order. By the end of the century, little indeed remained of the Knights except the name.

The twenty-five years from the start of the Civil War form an eventful period in the story of American labor. Rapid economic development caused many changes in the relationship between employer and employee, in the attitude of the skilled to the unskilled, and in the relative importance of national and local trade organization. Large corporations developed, particularly in railroads, mining, and iron and steel; their managers, dealing with vast masses of workers, could coldly plan how best to avoid the misfortune of unionism. A steel mill superintendent wrote in 1875:

We must be careful of what class of men we collect. We must steer clear of the West, where men are accustomed to infernal high wages. We must steer clear as far as we can of Englishmen who are great sticklers for high wages, small production and strikes. My experience has shown that Germans and Irish, Swedes and what I denominate "Buckwheats"—young American country boys, judiciously mixed, make the most effective and tractable force you can find.

Such deliberate policies of "judiciously mixing" the labor force, and of using recent immigrants or Negroes as strikebreakers, were not unsuccessful and helped to maintain that heterogeneity which, as in earlier periods, remained a marked feature of American labor. Statistics show, however, that only a very few foreign craftsmen were deliberately imported from abroad on contract to American manufacturers. The expense of the operation, and the readiness with which the imported craftsmen broke their contracts, account for this. At the same time, the influx of ordinary immigrants was so great that by 1870 the bulk of the labor force in most large cities was foreign-born. During the depression, immigration fell off; but its resumption at a high level in the 1880's went far to make up for the temporary loss.

That the working class consisted of unassimilated immigrants, that these immigrants had little direct contact with their employers in large-scale industry, and that they lived in slum districts quite separate from the rest of the community— all these factors account for the loss of status which manual labor suffered in this period. This was a psychological matter quite as much as an economic one. Taking the years 1860–85 as a whole, average real wages continued to increase, although the 1860's and the late 1870's were periods of retrogression, and some groups of workers, especially the unskilled and the women and children, suffered very much. At the same time, the traditional escape route of the artisan or laborer—to the West, and particularly into homestead farming—was probably operating less effectively than before the Civil War. Little good land remained for settlement when the special interests had been satisfied, and in any case the market for agricultural produce was already oversupplied by the later 1870's. In spite of the enormous growth of American industry, the great majority of the population still lived in the country or in towns of less than twenty-five hundred inhabitants; but as time went on the banks and railroads encroached upon the economic independence of the farmers and the rural communities, provoking that political alliance of rural and urban labor which found expression in the Greenback movement and in the variegated membership of the Knights of Labor.

The Knights aspired to unite the mass of the American people on a common platform of resistance to monopoly and a return to the old recognition of the dignity of labor. The mixed assemblies, which anyone could join except lawyers, gamblers, bankers, and liquor-dealers, were a form of organization that reflected the industrial character of the West, where there was little industrial concentration and where workers still moved readily from one type of job to another. The objects of the Order appealed strongly to those who were most downtrodden. It was significant that at its height about 10 per cent of the membership consisted of Negroes. Many of them were organized in separate assemblies because of the hostility of the white workers, especially in the South. But the principles of the Order discouraged discrimination, and the General Assembly held at Richmond, Virginia, in October, 1886, turned into something of a demonstration against the color bar. The real obstacle to the progress of the Knights, however, proved to lie in the suspicious exclusiveness of the skilled craftsmen of the East, or at least in that of the bulk of their trade-union leaders. Friction was bound to develop between them and any organization which sought to represent and even to control the whole world of American labor.

It was to be a long time, at least fifteen years, before the proportion of organized workers in the total labor force was to be as large as it had been in 1886, at the height of the popularity of the Knights. But the American Federation of Labor, which gradually took the lead from the Knights without ever exactly replacing them, was nevertheless much more soundly based and built to survive the stresses and strains of economic boom and slump. It is to an examination of its structure and its sources of strength, against the background of a new age, that we must now turn.

IV

Samuel Gompers, President

In 1886 Andrew Carnegie proclaimed in his *Triumphant Democracy:* "The old nations of the earth creep on at a snail's pace; the Republic thunders past with the speed of the express." These words, arrogant as they may seem, were in many ways substantially correct. Few indices of American industrial production failed to show a startling rate of growth in the last decades of the century, in spite of a serious depression in the mid-nineties. Immigration continued to stimulate the rapid increase of population, from about 50 million in 1880 to 76 million in 1900. New industries grew up to produce or to utilize new inventions—electric lighting and traction, the telephone, the typewriter, the adding machine. At the same time, the slightly older industries that had already developed into gigantic concerns, notably coal mining, railroads, iron and steel, meatpacking, and oil, became even more gigantic than before. Bituminous coal production expanded from 43 million tons in 1880 to 212 million in 1900, and anthracite from 30 million to 57 million. Pig iron output rose in the same period from less than 4 million to almost 14 million tons; steel production from 1.25 to over 10 million tons. Employment on the railroads rose by over a third in the 1890's alone, to reach over a million at the turn of the century.

The growth of the great industries was made even more impressive—not to say alarming—by the concentration of ownership and control that went on in each of them. By the early 1880's, observers of economic development were beginning to speak of "trusts" which owned vast sections of industry, in some cases to the point of monopoly. The first and best-known example was John D. Rockefeller's Standard Oil Company, which for a time won almost complete control of the petroleum industry. But the same process was soon at work in other fields. By the 1890's the bulk of the railroads had fallen into the hands of some half-dozen big financial groups, the largest of which were associated with the names of Morgan, Vanderbilt, and Harriman. The groups also had substantial holdings in the coal industry, as did the largest of the steel magnates. In steel, the outstanding name was that of Andrew Carnegie himself, who in association with H. C. Frick rapidly built up enormous interests in the Pittsburgh area, which were finally consolidated by J. P. Morgan at the turn of the century into the celebrated "billion dollar trust," the United States Steel Corporation.

These enterprises were so vast that they overshadowed many of the constitutional forms of government. They had such great economic power, for good or ill, that they could influence or even control state legislatures and could also carry great weight with Congress itself. They often encountered community opposition, especially in the more equalitarian West; but to counteract it they were prepared to supply their own private police, often obtained from the Pinkerton Agency, which specialized in this type of work. When Congress attempted to prevent the monopolies from growing too strong, notably by the Interstate Commerce Act of 1887 and by the Sherman Antitrust Act of 1890, their lawyers were able to find ways to avoid the more stringent provisions of the enactments, and the process of concentration went on much as before.

Owing to the rapidity of industrial growth and the great power of the so-called "robber barons" who directed it, there were few effective measures taken to insure the welfare and safety of the industrial worker. American industrial legislation lagged far behind that in major European countries, and the statistics showed an appalling injury rate in certain trades. In 1893, one of every 10 operating railroad employees was injured in some way, and one of every 115 was killed. In the Pennsylvania mines, one of every 150 was injured each year of the 1890's, and one of every 400 was killed. In the factories, machinery was not properly fenced to prevent accidents, yet child labor was limited in many states only by the requirements of school attendance—and these in turn were often lax.

Industrial conditions were no better, and in some ways worse, in the South. The section remained predominantly agricultural, and the number of tenant farmers rapidly increased in this period, bringing the total number of farms in the South from 1.5 million in 1880 to 2.5 million in 1900. But there were developments of industry in various areas—coal mining and iron and steel in Alabama, and textile manufacture more generally. Partly in order to attract industry, partly because it was as yet on a small scale, the industrial codes were even more lax than in the North. The extent of juvenile employment in the mills—which incidentally was almost always white labor—was so great that the Industrial Commission commented with resignation in 1901: "Perhaps the best that can be hoped for is the prohibition of child labor under the age of twelve in the Southern mills."

Such were the circumstances which the American Federation of Labor had to face in its early years. Its leaders had, indeed, the comparatively modest ambition of bringing the industrial legislation of the country up to the level of that in Britain and of securing trade-union rights as they had been secured by lobbying at Westminster. The structure of the American Federation was consciously modeled on that of the British Trades Union Congress, which allowed complete autonomy to its constituent bodies. And, like the British T.U.C., its appeal was at first largely restricted to craft unions, whose membership in proportion to the total labor force was much smaller than in Britain. So much for the myth that the Federation, by virtue of its structural similarity to the Constitution of the United States, was distinctively more "American" in its origin than the Knights of Labor.

At its first meeting in 1886 the Federation was provided with a very limited budget and with only one full-time officer. The latter was Samuel Gompers of the Cigar Makers, who was elected president. He was of Dutch-Jewish origin but had been born in London. The dues imposed upon member-unions of the Federation were to be no more than a quarter of a cent per capita every month—a figure which compared very unfavorably with the Knights' six cents every three months. Consequently, there was no question of the Federation being able to take much initiative in organizing or assisting strikes;

but the president and his part-time executive council were charged with the responsibility of encouraging the formation of local unions in trades still unorganized, central labor federations in cities where such bodies were not yet formed, and even national unions where the jurisdiction was unoccupied. To systematize these responsibilities, the Federation's officers were to issue "charters" of jurisdiction—a procedure which aroused some suspicion on the part of "strict constructionists" among the leaders of the founding unions, some of whom saw in it the seeds of a threat to their autonomy. The International Typographical Union, whose own locals retained much autonomy, insisted that the founding unions should be "affiliated" rather than "chartered"—a verbal change that was sanctioned by the convention of 1887.

Samuel Gompers himself as an opponent of the Knights of Labor had belonged to the "strict construction" school; and as leader of the Federation he realized the limits of his power. But the problems which he faced naturally led him to a more "national" standpoint, and he became an advocate of a central strike fund, such as the Knights had had. It was not surprising that he failed to get his way, and had to be content with a limited power of ordering special assessments to assist threatened unions. His position, then, was in modern terms more like that of the Secretary-General of the United Nations than like that of the President of the United States: he was an adviser and a reconciler, but he had very little executive power.

In this limited but important role, Gompers showed exceptional ability. He urged the unions to take a generous view of their responsibilities, but if he could not persuade them to go as far as he wished, he made the best of the situation as it was. He constantly urged the craft unions to recruit as many workers as possible in their trades, so that their exclusiveness would not weaken their industrial strength; and although he was not always successful in this, he at least had no grudge against industrial unions, two of which—the Mine Workers and the Brewery Workers—were by the end of the century among the six largest constituents of the Federation.

Gompers also sought to persuade the unions to accept Negro members, and for several years he pursued a policy of refusing unions admission to the Federation unless they removed all explicit discrimination from their national constitutions. This policy secured a token victory in 1895, when the International Association of Machinists entered the Federation on Gompers' terms after several years of obduracy; but the Machinists' locals continued to exclude Negroes, and so Gompers had achieved little by his attitude. He had also lost the affiliation of at least one of the railroad brotherhoods simply on this issue; and he seems to have decided in the 1890's that he had to be more flexible in the future, unless he were to sacrifice the strength of the Federation. By the end of the century he was even allowing the city central federations, over which he had rather more control, to exclude Negroes; and he was chartering separate colored federations to represent them.

Inevitably, Gompers and his colleagues on the executive council became involved in jurisdictional disputes between member unions and in disputes about whether unions seeking to join the Federation should be granted charters or should be regarded as "dual unions"—that is, illegal competitors working on the jurisdiction of unions already chartered. The heterogeneity of the American labor movement—caused, as we have seen, by ethnic differences, by variations in the mode of production, by absence of contacts between workers in different sections or regions—led to the growth of competing unions in many trades. The Brotherhood of Carpenters and Joiners, for instance, faced the competition of a union in the New York area called the United Order of Carpenters. It also encountered branches of the Amalgamated Society of Carpenters and Joiners, a union with headquarters at Manchester, England, whose American membership consisted almost entirely of British immigrants. In addition, the Brotherhood of Carpenters and Joiners quarreled constantly with the Machine Wood Workers and the Furniture Workers over the boundaries of their respective jurisdictions.

In many of these conflicts between the unions, Gompers was able to perform a valuable service of reconciliation. His skill as a negotiator, combined with his prestige as president of the Federation, enabled him to solve many disputes; and his letter books contain countless instances in which his wise advice and exhortation behind the scenes prevented open conflict. He secured the formation of several new national unions in the 1890's, among them the Electrical Workers, the Building Laborers, the Teamsters, and the Musicians. Sometimes, however, his hand was forced by the pressure of the unions that were already affiliated or chartered. The Brotherhood of Carpenters, for instance, was in an exceptionally strong position in the Federation, not only because of its size and strength, but because its secretary-treasurer, P. J. McGuire, was also an important officer of the Federation—originally secretary, then first vice-president. Consequently, when the Amalgamated Society of Carpenters and Joiners applied for a charter in 1888, it was at first denied; but when McGuire decided to reward the Amalgamated for its assistance in his fight with the United Order, the charter was at once granted. In later years, the Brotherhood was to turn against the Amalgamated once more and to secure the withdrawal of its charter.

The leading position of the Brotherhood of Carpenters inside the Federation was demonstrated in the new eight-hour agitation initiated by the Federation in 1890. It was Gompers' idea that each year one large union or trade should strike for the eight-hour day, with the financial support of all other unions. For 1890, the first year that this system was put into operation, the Carpenters were chosen to strike for the eight hours, and they did secure some substantial concessions. For 1891 it was to be the turn of the Mine Workers, but they proved to be too weak to take action, and the whole plan then collapsed. Gompers' designation of May 1, 1890, as the starting day of the movement led to the adoption of May Day as a special day of agitation by the Socialist International in Europe —an anniversary that has been marked ever since, and with special enthusiasm, ironically enough, by Socialists and Communists. For Gompers, as time went on, became more and more an opponent of Socialist influences in the labor movement, both inside the Federation and outside.

The organizations inside the Federation which were most involved with political affairs were the city federations, for they could mobilize votes much more easily than they could take industrial action. The largest of these bodies, especially those of New York and Chicago, could claim memberships that were much larger than those of nearly all the national or international unions. When the Federation was founded, they were just on the point of making their most convincing demonstrations of political strength. The failure of the strikes of 1886 led to a sudden revival of interest in labor politics, which culminated in the fall of that year. In New York, Henry George, the "single tax" advocate, was selected as a "Labor Party" candidate for the office of mayor, and he was backed by the New York Central Labor Union, by the Knights of Labor, and by a wide range of political groups including the Socialists. He was not elected, but he ran second and secured a total of sixty-seven thousand votes. At Chicago, a similar "United Labor Party" elected a number of judges for Cook County and also a state senator and six state assemblymen. But after this, the apparent unity of labor began to disintegrate in both cities. Henry George quarreled with the Socialists, and they were expelled from the New York United Labor Party. George was nominated for secretary of state of New York in 1887, but this time he ran a poor third, losing half his city vote of 1886. In Chicago a secession to the Democratic party led to a similar decline of strength at the polls.

It was clear that the urban workers only allowed their feelings of class solidarity to unite them for a brief period. As soon as that period was over, ethnic rivalries reasserted themselves. It must be remembered that occupation was also to a large extent determined by national origin at this time. The most highly skilled workers—railroad engineers and printers for instance—tend to be predominantly American-born. The older immigrants, Irish and German, dominated the building trades, and the Germans were well established in cigar-making, brewing, and furniture work. The lake seamen of Chicago were Scandinavian, the apartment janitors Flemish. The humbler and less well-paid jobs necessarily went to the most recent immigrants, many of whom in the 1890's came from eastern and southern Europe, one-third to one-half of them being illiterate and very few of them having any industrial skills. The Jews tended to concentrate in the clothing trades, in which they had been established in Europe, and worked in "sweated" conditions for miserable wages. Being both more educated and more radical than the other new immigrants they soon developed an interest in labor organization, but they formed their separate Jewish unions, which in New York were united in a body called the United Hebrew Trades. The Czechs, the Poles, and the Italians also crowded into the big cities and were available for all types of unskilled work. Because they found it difficult to communicate with earlier immigrants or with the native Americans, they could readily be used as strikebreakers.

Such being the state of affairs in the large cities, it is not surprising that it was difficult to keep the union locals together in one form of central organization. In 1888 the New York Socialists, who were mostly of German or other foreign-language origin, organized a rival to the Central Labor Union, which they called the Central Labor Federation. Both these bodies secured charters from the American Federation of Labor; and Gompers was instrumental in reconciling them and persuading them to unite in 1889. But this unity did not last: in 1890 the Central Labor Federation was reformed and applied for the restoration of its charter. Gompers, however, rejected the application this time, on the grounds that a section of the Socialist Labor Party was formally affiliated with it as a constituent body. Gompers had no objection to Socialists participating in the work of a city federation, provided that they did so as union representatives; but he opposed the representation of a political party as such inside a trade-union organization. The Socialist Labor Party, which had an extremely doctrinaire leadership, proved obdurate, and the matter was debated for a day and a half at the ensuing convention of the American Federation of Labor. The delegates upheld Gompers' attitude by a substantial majority.

This conflict was an important one partly because it threw Gompers, who was as yet by no means an anti-Socialist, into a defensive attitude against the Socialist movement; but also because, owing to the uncompromising tactics of their leaders, it alienated a substantial section of the Socialists altogether from the A.F. of L. This may have been decisive in 1893 and 1894, when a radical political program was under discussion at the A.F. of L. conventions. The program was introduced in 1893 by Thomas J. Morgan, a Chicago machinist, who was an admirer of the comparatively moderate British socialists. His proposals contained eleven planks, number ten of which was "The collective ownership by the people of all means of production and distribution." The program was not accepted at the 1893 convention, but came up for further discussion a year later and was finally defeated only after long and vigorous debate.

At both conventions Gompers had strongly criticized the Socialists, and in 1894 this led to his own defeat in the election for president for the ensuing year. Gompers' successful rival was John McBride, president of the United Mine Workers, who was not himself a Socialist, but who benefited from the Socialists' hostility to Gompers. McBride turned out to be a poor substitute for Gompers as principal officer of the Federation; he was rude to other union leaders, and so lost support. Gompers was re-elected in 1895 by a narrow margin and thereafter secured annual re-election until his death in the 1920's.

Meanwhile the Socialist Labor Party, alienated from the A.F. of L., had thrown its forces into the task of winning control of the Knights of Labor through the agency of District Assembly 49. We have already mentioned that Powderly was overthrown in 1893 by a combination of New York Socialists and western radicals, whose representative, James R. Sovereign, was elected in his place. But the Socialist Labor Party was not strong enough to overcome Sovereign and his supporters, and the upshot of their conflict was the expulsion of the Socialists from the Order in 1895. Daniel De Leon, who had emerged as the dominant leader of the Socialist Labor Party, now established an independent Socialist Trade and Labor Alliance which was to be a rival to both the A.F. of L. and the Knights. This was a deliberate policy of "dual unionism" which many of the Socialists themselves, especially those outside New York, could not approve of. Its principal result, in fact, was (to coin a phrase) "dual Socialism"; various groups of Socialists who disapproved of De Leon's policy founded a rival organization, the Social Democracy, at a convention in Chicago in 1897. This body, which included nearly all the English-speaking Socialists, made rapid progress, and in 1900 it united with a moderate section of the Socialist Labor Party to form a new organization, the Socialist Party of America, which soon became much the largest Socialist party in the United States.

The largest group of organized workers who did not belong to the American Federation of Labor was to be found in the railroad industry. We have already mentioned that one railroad union was denied membership in the Federation because of the "white clause" in its constitution; this was the Brotherhood of Locomotive Firemen, which was considering affiliation in 1896. Many of the other railroad brotherhoods had similar clauses, and the same factor must have militated against their joining the Federation. But there were other reasons. The brotherhoods were very exclusive bodies, rarely willing to collaborate with one another, and unlike most labor organizations they regarded their insurance functions as being more important than their functions as collective bargaining agents. The Order of Railway Conductors, in fact, in this period refused to accept the view that it had any collective bargaining functions at all. These attitudes derived from the high standards of skill and discipline required for those who operated the trains, from their success in actually obtaining significant wage differentials, and from their constant heavy rates of accidents, injuries, and deaths.

The exclusive attitudes of the railroad brotherhoods gave rise to a great deal of rivalry, not merely between their members and other railroad workers, such as the switchmen, who were less skilled, less well paid, and less organized, but also within themselves and between the brotherhoods and their unorganized colleagues in the same crafts. Friction of this type gravely weakened them in the struggles of this period, especially as the railroad companies were themselves beginning to co-ordinate their labor policies and particularly their action in the face of a strike against one or more of their number. In 1886 a General Managers Association was formed at Chicago, to deal with all matters of common interest affecting the railroad companies which served that important junction. It was, in fact, a strike in the Chicago neighborhood in the spring of that year which led to the foundation of the Association.

The most important railroad labor disputes of the period were the Burlington strike of 1888 and the Pullman boycott of 1894, both of which directly concerned Chicago and the lines in the Association. The Burlington strike was in origin a strike of locomotive engineers and firemen, and it was organized by a grievance committee of Burlington employees, rather than by the national officers of the brotherhoods, who disapproved of the whole venture. The strikers were aided by the fact that the General Managers Association failed to function, many of the other companies apparently regarding this as a good opportunity to capture the business of the line. But they were hindered by the fact that scab engineers and firemen were quickly recruited by the company, partly from the conductors and trainmen who felt no sympathy for their fellow employees and partly from engineers and firemen unemployed since the Gould strikes, for whose failure they blamed the brotherhoods. Attempts to enforce the strike by a secondary boycott of Burlington cargoes on other roads at first received tacit encouragement from the managers of some of the other companies, but the boycott was soon broken by injunctions secured by the Burlington company.

Members of the brotherhoods realized why their strike on the Burlington had failed, and a movement for federation of the brotherhoods emerged as a result. But the movement was no great success; conservative forces soon reasserted themselves in the leadership of the Locomotive Engineers, where the authority of P. M. Arthur as "Grand Chief Engineer" was fully restored. It was left to the militant former secretary of the Locomotive Firemen, Eugene V. Debs, to attempt an entirely new form of organization—an industrial union recruiting all railroad workers, with the name of American Railway Union, which he formed in 1893. This union sought to supplant the brotherhoods altogether, as well as to draw into the same organization the workers which the brotherhoods had always ignored—switchmen, maintenance workers, and indeed all who worked for the railroad companies in any capacity.

Unfortunately for Debs, 1893 and the immediately succeeding years did not provide a suitable environment for the infancy of a highly militant industrial organization. A financial panic occurred in 1893 and four years of depression followed, in the course of which the labor force on the railroads was considerably reduced. Before 1893 was out, unemployment was estimated at some two million or more; and early in 1894, desperate bands of workers, including railroad men, were making their way to Washington from different parts of the country to demand relief. The idea of a march to Washington was initiated by one Jacob S. Coxey, and the first group of some hundred marchers, who set out from his home in Ohio, were known as "Coxey's Army." But other "armies" were to follow, especially from the Far West, and although the numbers involved were not large—probably not more than ten thousand all told—the movement had sufficient news value to attract constant attention. The western contingents obtained a good deal of support from public opinion and even from the local authorities; and they often commandeered locomotives and coaches on the railroads, finding engineers and firemen from their own ranks. When the various "armies" straggled into Washington, they were not allowed to present their petitions in person to the President or to Congress, and, in the face of strong police forces, they could do nothing but stay in encampments or go home. Some of them stayed for a time, but the movement ended in anticlimax as their numbers gradually dwindled.

During this period—the spring and early summer of 1894—there was a good deal of labor unrest, but there were too many unemployed to make it easy for a new union to take the offensive. In April, however, the American Railway Union did win a strike on the Great Northern Railroad; and the prestige that accrued to it as a result enabled it to build up its membership to something like 150,000. It probably needed a period of consolidation before engaging in any further disputes; but it was diffcult to pursue a policy of caution when its members were inclined to go on strike of their own accord, as happened with the Pullman workers in the summer of 1894. Public opinion sided strongly with the employees of the Pullman Palace Car Company, whose wages were cut severely but whose rents in the "model" company town just south of Chicago remained at the same high level. The Pullman Company could close down its manufacturing works without serious loss, for it continued to draw a steady revenue from the rolling stock that it had hired to the railroad companies. In order to assist the Pullman strikers, the American Railway Union instituted a boycott of the Pullman cars on the railroads.

Four main factors contributed to the failure of this boycott and to the resultant collapse of the American Railway Union. The first has already been suggested: where railroad employees went on strike, it was not difficult for the managers to find replacements in the existing state of reduced employment. A second factor was the hostility of the brotherhoods to the new union, which they realized was designed to replace their own organizations. They therefore did nothing to discourage their members from taking jobs vacated by strikers. Third, the companies, realizing that Debs's union constituted the most dangerous challenge to their authority that they had yet had to face, co-operated closely through the General Managers' Association. Fourth—and this was decisive—the federal gov-

Terence V. Powderly. (Courtesy, Chicago Historical Society.)

Samuel Gompers. (Courtesy, ate Historical Society, Wisconsin.)

In eight languages, the steel employers urge a resumption of work during the 1919 strike.

ernment, in the person of Richard Olney, President Cleveland's Attorney General, stepped in swiftly to secure injunctions against the interruption of the movement of mail and interstate commerce; and to enforce these injunctions, he prevailed upon Cleveland to send in federal troops. Gompers and the A.F. of L., though not unsympathetic, could do virtually nothing to help the American Railway Union; and the strike soon collapsed. Debs and a number of his colleagues were indicted for violating the injunctions, and Debs himself was sentenced to a six-month prison term.

With the failure of the Pullman strike, all hope of creating a comprehensive industrial union on the railroads was extinguished. The brotherhoods resumed their efforts to form a federation, but disagreements arose between them once more, and by the turn of the century they were working as independently as ever. The strength of craft consciousness had thus triumphed over industrial militancy or class consciousness; and it had been powerfully assisted by the unity of the railroad managers and by the federal government's prompt intervention. The injunction proved to be a valuable and effective way of restraining strikers; it saved time, and it avoided recourse to a jury, which was more likely to sympathize with strikers than a judge, particularly a federal judge. By a curious irony, the most effective type of injunction for use against the union turned out to be based on the Sherman Antitrust Act of 1890, which declared illegal any combination or conspiracy in restraint of trade between the states. Only effective political pressure by a united labor movement could alter this interpretation of the law; but the brotherhoods, at least, seemed unwilling to join with their fellow workers to secure this end.

American Labor

If the American Federation of Labor had a very limited foothold in the railroad industry, it was all the more important for it to achieve some strength in the two other major industries, coal mining and steel. The National Federation of Miners and Mine Laborers—clearly intended to be an industrial rather than purely a craft union—was formed by John McBride in Ohio in 1885, and it joined the A.F. of L. at its foundation in 1886. For the first four years it had to face the opposition of a rival body organized by the Knights of Labor; but in 1890 an amalgamation took place, and the United Mine Workers of America came into existence. After its first two years of existence, the united organization had a membership of only about twenty thousand; and the ensuing depression reduced the numbers still further, to about ten thousand in 1896. Wages were already very low, owing to the introduction of new immigrant labor, much of it Italian or Slav in origin; and in 1897 they were still further reduced. At this point the union, under the leadership of Michael Ratchford, made a last desperate stand, and ordered a general stoppage in the bituminous mines. The order was unexpectedly successful: altogether a hundred thousand miners came out on strike in support of the union. As it happened, business was beginning to pick up and the demand for coal was increasing. The operators therefore came to terms with the union, and a compromise wage scale was agreed upon. The following year this was elaborated into an interstate agreement to equalize wage scales in Ohio, Illinois, Indiana, and western Pennsylvania.

In 1899, John Mitchell, a national organizer of the union who had proved his worth in the course of the strike, was elected president at the age of twenty-nine. The membership of the union was now rising rapidly; it passed the hundred thousand mark in 1900, when Mitchell initiated a strike in the anthracite field. Here again, large numbers of unorganized workers joined the minority of union members to insure success; and here too, membership in the union rapidly shot up, so that the total in 1901 was verging upon two hundred thousand. The American Federation benefited considerably from this great advance, not merely because the Mine Workers were affiliated so that any increase in their strength was an increase in that of the Federation, but also because Gompers and the executive council had made a considerable contribution to the rebuilding of the miners' union, by personal agitation, by sending in organizers, and by making donations from the Federation's funds.

The adhesion of the Mine Workers to the American Federation of Labor, and their growing strength, was compensation for the decline of the Federation's support in the steel industry. At the beginning of the 1890's the Amalgamated Association of Iron, Steel, and Tin Workers, which was an affiliate of the A.F. of L., claimed a total of over twenty-four thousand members, which was about a quarter of those eligible to belong. It was, however, a union which restricted its membership to skilled workers in the industry, and it did not recruit the increasing force of unskilled laborers. In 1892, H. C. Frick, who was managing the Carnegie works at Homestead, Pennsylvania, ordered a reduction of wages, and the entire labor force went on strike. Frick reacted by recruiting a force of some three hundred Pinkerton guards and having them sent in by night on river barges. But the river convoy did not take the strikers unawares, and as the guards tried to land, a battle broke out which resulted in the death of nine workers and three Pinkertons. After thirteen hours the Pinkertons surrendered, and the strike went on. The National Guard of Pennsylvania moved in, and under their protection strikebreakers were introduced, and the works restarted on a non-union basis. The strike dragged on for several months, but finally ended in complete defeat, only a few of the strikers being taken back by the company. The Amalgamated Association of Iron, Steel, and Tin Workers suffered an almost fatal blow as a result, for it lost members in many other plants, and by 1895 its membership had fallen to less than half of the 1891 figure.

Clearly there was little that the union could do to rebuild its strength in the period of the depression of 1893–97. As soon as prosperity returned, it found itself faced by managements which were rapidly being consolidated into the largest single industrial concern in the world—the United States Steel Corporation, which was formed in 1901. Since a number of mills controlled by the Corporation were entirely free of unionization, it was clear that the Amalgamated Association was in a very weak position vis-à-vis the new corporation—especially as the introduction of new mechanical processes lessened the need for skilled men of the type that were admitted to the union.

The initial policy of the Corporation was to accept the existing extent of union organization, at least for the time being, but to oppose its extension. But in negotiating an agreement with some of the Corporation's subsidiaries in 1901, the union under the lead of President T. J. Shaffer insisted on a uniform scale for all the mills of the companies concerned, fearing that otherwise they would eventually be forced out of the companies' works by the switching of contracts to non-union mills. In July, 1901, a strike began, and in the following month it developed into a general strike against the United

States Steel Corporation as a whole. Over sixty thousand men came out, which showed that the union did not lack support outside its own membership; and the Corporation made a compromise offer which the Amalgamated Association rejected, although Gompers advised acceptance. After this, however, the strike rapidly weakened, and in September the Amalgamated was forced to come to terms, losing fourteen mills where it had members and being forced to recognize the limitation of its membership to the remainder.

This was a very serious setback because it meant the virtual end of unionism in the steel industry. The Amalgamated Association had little left except its hold in the iron mills. President Shaffer, evidently seeking a scapegoat for his own misjudgment, blamed Gompers and Mitchell of the Mine Workers for failing to come to his assistance. In fact, neither of these leaders could have done much to help; Mitchell could hardly have been expected to bring out his men in a sympathetic strike so shortly after their own exhausting struggles had come to an end. The Amalgamated Association certainly had a difficult situation to face; but it made its own position worse—first, by failing to organize all types of workers in the mills, and second, by rejecting a reasonable temporary settlement when offered it during the dispute.

In 1901 the membership of the American Federation of Labor was nearing the million mark, which was well over three times as large as it had been as recently as 1898. The Knights of Labor probably did not amount to more than 200,-000, and the railroad brotherhoods had 165,000. A number of other independent unions, mostly small, brought the total of all organized workers to about 1,400,000. If we take the nonagricultural labor force, including salaried workers and self-employed, to amount to nineteen million altogether, and if we allow a small proportion for Canadian membership, we find that approximately one out of every fourteen workers belonged to unions at this time. This was a larger figure than ever before, but it still did not amount to very much and it compared unfavorably with the ratio in Britain, which was roughly twice as large.

At least Gompers could be satisfied that the American Federation of Labor had no effective rival for national leadership of the movement. As the affiliated membership of the Federation was still rising rapidly, he could look forward with some confidence to the future. At the same time, there were serious weaknesses in his position. The trend of the times seemed to be toward larger and larger concentrations of industrial power, and it was precisely in the plants owned by these great concentrations that the Federation was most unsuccessful. The miners, it is true, had reasserted themselves triumphantly; but the industrial solidarity produced in mining communities was something exceptional, and the bulk of the Federation's member unions were craft organizations which seemed quite as vulnerable as the Amalgamated Association of Iron, Steel, and Tin Workers. The Federation was also very weak in the West; the union of the metal miners of the Rocky Mountain area, the Western Federation of Miners, spurned association with the A.F. of L. and even launched an organization designed to do its work in the West. This, the Western Labor Union, was no great success, but it indicated the strength of sectional rivalries inside the labor movement; and there were always elements elsewhere—the Knights of Labor, the Socialists, and the independent unions which either had never sought an A.F. of L. charter or had been denied one—available to form the nucleus of a rival federation.

Gompers was also concerned to acquire more status for the labor movement with the employers. He wanted to educate them to accept the view that a responsible trade-union movement was an asset to an industrial enterprise rather than a liability. This was an uphill task, for most employers accepted the strict economic standpoint that the value of labor must be measured by supply and demand alone, and that insofar as the unions tried to limit the supply, their influence was necessarily nefarious. One means of influence which Gompers sought to make use of was the National Civic Federation, an organization founded in 1900 to bring together various leaders of the community in order to avoid social unrest and disturbances. This body, which won the support of a number of business leaders and professional people, mostly in the East, was at first regarded with some suspicion by the labor leaders, but the fact that the more uncompromising captains of industry regarded it as a deplorable concession to labor encouraged Gompers and his immediate colleagues to make use of it with more confidence. Under its first president, Senator Mark Hanna, it began to influence public opinion toward accepting collective bargaining in industry.

The A.F. of L. also concerned itself, as the Knights of Labor had done, with immigration, which served to keep up a constant supply of labor and so to weaken the position of the unions. The immigrants of the late 1880's and the 1890's, less assimilable and less educated than those who had come before, were the cause of widespread demands for restrictions, often on the grounds of racial theory which was then becoming increasingly current. Workingmen were by no means immune to arguments of this type, it need hardly be said, and the nativist American Protective Association, which was formed in 1887, had a substantial amount of labor support.

In 1892 the Knights of Labor, which had helped to secure the law against the importation of labor by contract, came out in favor of a general restriction of immigration. In the mid-1890's, a number of states passed laws prohibiting the employment of aliens on state and local public works—measures which can only have been passed under pressure from organized labor. Yet the American Federation of Labor moved slowly on this question, partly because Gompers and several other members of the leadership were themselves first-generation immigrants—Gompers having the additional characteristic that, like many of the new immigrants, he was a Jew. In 1897 a committee of the A.F. of L. reported in favor of a proposal to introduce a literacy test, and this was accepted by the convention. In later years, when the membership of the Federation came to consist more largely of native Americans, its attitude to immigration was gradually to stiffen in the direction of more restrictive measures.

V

Trusts, Socialists, and Wobblies

By the end of the nineteenth century the United States was already the richest country in the world, and her industry the most powerful. The rapid expansion which had enabled her to attain this position continued throughout the first two decades of the twentieth century and can readily be measured from the indices of production, of increasing urbanization, and of population growth. The total value of manufactured products more than doubled between 1899 and 1919; the proportion of the population living in cities and towns of more than twenty-five hundred people rose from 29.7 per cent to 51.4 per cent between 1900 and 1920; and the total number of inhabitants of the continental United States rose from 76 million to 106.5 million. Further evidence of the increasing maturity of the country's economy was provided by the growth of manufactured exports and of overseas investments. Between 1898 and 1914 the former almost trebled, the latter multiplied fivefold.

American Labor

These early years of the century witnessed the last great waves of transatlantic migration. Numerically, the movement transcended all those that had preceded it, for in several individual years the annual total exceeded one million. The aggregate of immigrants entering the United States between 1901 and 1915—when the World War cut off the means of transportation—was about 11.5 million. Proportionately to the existing population of the United States, this influx was not quite as large as it had been in the early 1850's, just after the European potato famine. All the same, it was very considerable, and it gave rise to fierce controversy over proposals for restriction. Most of the newcomers were from the Mediterranean lands or from eastern Europe: Slavs from the Russian Empire or from Austria-Hungary numbered over four million; Italians, mostly from southern Italy or Sicily, amounted to over three million; and Jews, nearly all of them from Russia, totaled almost one and a half million.

The effect of this heavy immigration was, inevitably, to prevent average real wages from rising as they would otherwise have done. This was a period of rising prices, and wages did no more than keep pace with them, in spite of the enormous increases of productivity which were taking place simultaneously. It was fortunate, however, that there was little severe unemployment in these years. A sharp setback to trade took place in 1908–9 and again in 1914, and on both occasions the unemployment figures temporarily rose above two million. But every other year was a record year in the physical output of manufactures, and the general level of employment was high. Agriculture was prosperous throughout the period, and farm values increased considerably. Although some concern was expressed at the growth of tenancy, notably in the

Middle West, there could be no doubt that it was easier than it had been to make a living from the land.

The South still continued, however, to lie outside the main stream of social and economic development. The sharecropping system held the Negro in bondage to the soil; and although illiteracy was being conquered gradually, opportunities of economic advancement for either race were very limited. The pattern of segregation was still developing, and after the emergence of the Populist movement in the southern states in the early 1890's, various means were found to complete the disfranchisement of the Negro. In spite of the policy of acquiescence preached by Booker T. Washington, the Negro leader, and widely accepted by the colored population, white supremacy apparently needed to be frequently asserted by violent means: lynchings averaged about 150 a year in the 1890's and continued in the following decade at a little less than a hundred a year. Northerners, obsessed with the problems presented by imperialism abroad and by immigration at home, paid little attention to this situation; but in 1909 a small but important beginning was made by the foundation, largely under northern white leadership, of the National Association for the Advancement of Colored People.

As we have seen, the prosperity of the years after 1897 enormously increased the strength of American trade unionism, so that already by 1901 the total membership was reported to the Industrial Commission as being nearly one and a half million. This may well have been an exaggeration at the time, but if so it soon achieved reality as the expansion continued; and conservative estimates put the total at two million in 1904, which was four times the figure of 1898. About four-fifths of this total were affiliated to the American Federation of Labor. One of the largest beneficiaries of the growth was the United Mine Workers, which in 1902 consolidated itself by winning a protracted strike in the anthracite fields—a conflict of national importance which ended with the intervention of President Roosevelt and the appointment by him of a commission to settle the dispute. John Mitchell's cautious leadership of the miners helped to win over public opinion to their side, and the commission recognized that the union had a case. It recommended a new agreement making some concessions to the miners. The newly organized National Civic Federation played a part in resolving the issue, and thereby won Mitchell as one of its keenest adherents. The role of the federal government in the dispute was an entirely novel one and an important precedent for the future.

But the National Civic Federation, with its policy of union recognition and conciliation, secured the support of only a section of the employers of the country. The National Association of Manufacturers, under its president, David M. Parry, decided to fight back against the recognition of trade unionism. Already at Dayton, Ohio, at Beloit, Wisconsin, and at Chicago local employers' associations had been campaigning successfully against the closed shop, which union leaders regarded as an essential of effective union security. The issue suited the employers, because it enabled them to assume the role of defenders of individual liberty. In reality, however, in a situation where immigrant labor, ignorant of the English language and of trade-union practice, could at once be brought in to compete with union labor, the restoration of the open shop very often meant the end of effective unionism.

Trusts, Socialists, and Wobblies

The open-shop campaign aroused immediate enthusiasm among employers throughout the country. In 1903 Parry founded a new organization, the Citizens' Industrial Association, to organize the campaign nationally. Many local associations were formed, and soon the unions found their outposts in the smaller industrial towns being whittled away, while even in larger cities membership began to decline as union shops became non-union. Outside the conflict, public opinion often favored the apparent defenders of freedom; and President Charles W. Eliot of Harvard went so far as to acclaim the strikebreaker in general as "a very good type of modern hero." The National Association of Manufacturers also asserted itself to nullify the lobbying efforts of labor organizations at Washington and to defeat at the polls any congressmen who showed themselves too friendly to labor.

At this time a number of important labor cases were on their way through the courts. In 1903 a firm of hatters, D. E. Loewe and Company of Danbury, Connecticut, sued the officers and members of the hatters' union for the sum of $240,000, which they claimed under the Sherman Act as triple damages for losses incurred as the result of a boycott of their products. In February, 1908, the Supreme Court upheld the prosecution as justified under the Sherman Act, and later a jury allowed the full amount of damages claimed. Another boycott case, initiated by the Bucks' Stove and Range Company in 1907, directly affected Gompers and the other officers of the A.F. of L., for the company secured an injunction against them when they included its name on the "unfair list" published in the *American Federationist*, the monthly A.F. of L. journal. Gompers and his colleagues ignored the injunction and again included the company in the list;

and as a result they were cited for contempt of court in 1909. Gompers himself was sentenced to a prison term; and the conviction hung over his head for a number of years, but in 1914 it was finally quashed on a technicality. In these two cases, the issues were pressed by employers closely linked with the national campaign against unionism. D. E. Loewe had helped to form an Anti-Boycott Association in 1902; and J. W. Van Cleave, the president of the Buck's Stove and Range Company, was Parry's successor as president of the National Association of Manufacturers.

Meanwhile the United States Steel Corporation had decided to eliminate the last vestiges of unionism from its subsidiaries. Late in 1902 it instituted a profit-sharing plan, apparently with the object of binding its employees more closely to their jobs; and in 1909 the last of its unionized mills were declared open shops. The union concerned, the Amalgamated Association, called a last-ditch strike, which gathered strength when many non-union men joined it and which dragged on for fourteen months. But in spite of full support from Gompers and financial assistance from the A.F. of L. in the form of a per capita levy on all members, the workers were completely defeated. At about the same time, the Lake Seamen's Union was crushed by the Lake Carriers' Association, which was virtually an agent of the steel magnates. One remarkable feature of both these strikes was that the employers were in each case offering an increase of wages at the time. The sole issue of conflict was the recognition of the union.

Yet another union whose position was threatened by U.S. Steel through one of its subsidiaries was the Bridge and Structural Iron Workers, which was faced with an open-shop drive by the National Erectors Association. Being hard pressed, the union fell into the hands of two desperate men, Frank M. Ryan and John J. McNamara, who resorted to the use of dynamite against buildings constructed by non-union labor. In October, 1910, the Los Angeles *Times* building was blown up with the loss of twenty lives—an outrage which shocked the whole country and which Gompers refused to believe could have been the work of union men. The fact that Mc-Namara, who was at Indianapolis, was promptly kidnaped by private detectives and taken to California under duress, made Gompers all the more anxious to insure that the case was properly defended. In consultation with his colleagues, he therefore secured the well-known defense attorney Clarence Darrow as chief counsel, and guaranteed payment of costs on behalf of the A.F. of L. A special "McNamara Defense Committee" was set up with Frank Morrison, the A.F. of L. secretary, in charge. To the acute embarrassment of the con-servative labor leaders, however, McNamara and his brother, who was also on trial, pleaded guilty on the advice of their counsel. This turn of events (in December, 1911) and the subsequent conviction of other officers of the union for con-spiracy were heavy blows to the public reputation of the labor movement, which Gompers had for so long been pain-fully trying to build up.

Meanwhile the A.F. of L. was being challenged on its flank by the formation of a rival national labor organization. The Western Federation of Miners had for some time been hostile to the type of unionism represented by the A.F. of L. The concepts of craft exclusiveness and autonomy, and the at-tempt to secure mutual respect between employer and em-ployee, seemed quite out of place in the mining camps of

American Labor

Colorado and Idaho, where law enforcement was so inadequate that labor disputes readily degenerated into civil wars. The Western Labor Union, which as we have seen was founded by the Western Federation of Miners, was designed to comprise all the workers of the West, "irrespective of occupation, nationality, creed or color." The new organization made little progress, but in 1902 it was decided to extend its scope, with the intention, as the union journal put it, of forcing "the Gompers brigade" to "keep step to the music of progress" or alternatively, of eliminating "this per capita tax eating gang from the councils of organized labor." The headquarters of the Western Labor Union were moved from Butte to Chicago and its name was changed to American Labor Union.

In 1904 the Western Federation of Miners was weakened by the complete defeat of its strike at Cripple Creek, Colorado, by a combination of forces led by the Mine Owners' Association and local Citizens' Alliances. Its members in the area were simply driven away and replaced by foreign immigrants and country boys. The miners' leaders turned more and more to the prospect of help from a strong new national organization. Meetings were held in Chicago to plan the formation of such a body, and a number of prominent Socialists were drawn in, including Eugene V. Debs, the former president of the American Railway Union, who was now the most popular spokesman of the Socialist Party of America. Daniel De Leon and his Socialist Trade and Labor Alliance also found the new venture to their taste, and rallied to its assistance.

The delegates who met at Chicago in June, 1905, to found the Industrial Workers of the World (soon abbreviated to I.W.W.) represented almost all the forces of labor which, whether for temporary or for permanent reasons, resented the domination of the A.F. of L. in the labor movement. They did not, however, include the highly conservative railroad brotherhoods. Debs and his colleagues represented the current of hostility to conservative unionism which existed in the Socialist Party of America—although it is true that many preferred to work through the A.F. of L. and opposed this attempt to found a rival union organization. De Leon, the Socialist Labor Party and the Socialist Trade and Labor Alliance were of course happy to find allies in the work of "smashing" the A.F. of L. The only union of any size which committed itself to joining the new body was the Western Federation of Miners; but one somewhat unexpected ally was the Amalgamated Society of Engineers, a tiny body consisting mostly of immigrants who were members of the British union of that name, and who were nursing a grudge against the A.F. of L., from which they had lately been unceremoniously expelled at the behest of their stronger rivals, the Machinists. Thus ethnic and sectional factors combined to add weight to a protest movement which, superficially at least, seemed almost entirely ideological in character.

The attitude of the I.W.W. was stated boldly in the first sentence of the preamble to its constitution: "The working class and the employing class have nothing in common." Its object was to unite the workers in one centralized organization, without distinction of trade, skill, race, or ethnic origin. Initiation fees and dues were to be kept to the minimum so that no one would be excluded on grounds of poverty. The only division among the members was to be on industrial lines, for there were to be thirteen departments of the I.W.W. covering all the possible occupations of the workers; but the

I.W.W. executive board was to have the authority to call any section of the organization out on strike. All this was accepted enthusiastically by the inaugural convention, but there was some difference of opinion on the value of political action, which some of the delegates thought was an undesirable diversion from industrial work. A clause indorsing the use of political action was carried by a majority.

In nearly all respects the I.W.W. was the exact antithesis of the A.F. of L., as indeed it was designed to be. Centralization contrasted with the national-union autonomy of the older body; industrial organization cut across the craft basis of the A.F. of L. unions; and the policy of low dues differed markedly from the high-contribution systems which Gompers and his colleagues favored. But the I.W.W. had even more difficulty than the A.F. of L. in deciding its attitude to politics, and this soon led to factionalism within its ranks. At the second convention in 1906, De Leon and his group secured the defeat of those leaders of the Western Federation of Miners who opposed political action. This was a very damaging act, as it led to the withdrawal of the Western Federation of Miners from the I.W.W., which deprived it of the bulk of its membership. At the same time, Debs and several other prominent Socialists dropped out, being disappointed at the new turn of events. There were, however, two Western Federation leaders still left in, and both of them were men of distinct personality—William D. Haywood and Vincent St. John; and the I.W.W. itself consisted not only of the dogmatic De Leonites but also of an unruly band of western "hoboes," unskilled in the dialectics of Socialist theory but willing to follow any effective leadership. St. John, who had himself been something of a "hobo," mobilized the western elements and in 1908 was able to drive De Leon out of the organization and to abolish the clause in the constitution which favored political action. De Leon, refusing to accept defeat, established a rival I.W.W. at Detroit with the political clause still retained, but this body never acquired any influence of note.

Under St. John, who was secretary-treasurer from 1908 to 1915, the Chicago I.W.W. gradually attained national prominence, if not large membership. Most of its work was done either among the migratory workers of the West or among the unskilled immigrants of the eastern cities. In the West, the I.W.W. recruited lumber workers and farm laborers and mobilized them for the violent battles into which western labor disputes almost inevitably degenerated. They engaged in campaigns for "free speech," and met the challenge of the vigilantes organized by the local property owners. In the East, their role was different: they provided an English-speaking leadership for groups of immigrant workers, notably for those in the textile factories, who found themselves neglected by the small and conservative A.F. of L. union of their trade, the United Textile Workers. The largest and most important of their strikes was that at Lawrence, Massachusetts, in 1912, when under the leadership of Joseph J. Ettor and Bill Haywood some thirty thousand workers won wage increases and other benefits.

But the "Wobblies" (as the members of the I.W.W. were commonly called) secured little permanent increase of membership as the result of their efforts. Their tactics and methods of propaganda, including the open advocacy of sabotage (a word derived from the French Syndicalists), were too extreme for all save the most desperate workers to accept. Haywood himself, who was a member of the National Executive of the Socialist Party, was deprived of that office by national referendum of the party for his advocacy of violence. Another factor which prevented the I.W.W. from gathering real strength was the indiscipline of its members, who refused to acknowledge the necessity for central control. By 1914, Debs, who had continued to look upon the I.W.W. with a good deal of sympathy, was at last convinced that it "stands for anarchy," and was prepared to advocate a fresh start in revolutionary unionism, based upon the two miners' unions, the Western Federation and the United Mine Workers. Ten years after its foundation, the membership of the I.W.W. was apparently hovering round about the 15,000 mark, which was less than one-hundredth of the membership of the A.F. of L.

The importance of the I.W.W. was much more symbolical than actual. It was a protest against the A.F. of L.'s claim to speak for a working class which consisted to an increasing extent of unskilled workers, whether native or immigrant. Although some of its leaders were influenced by Marxism and by Syndicalism, it was nevertheless largely the product of the American environment. The Wobblies fit naturally into the mythology of the West, along with the cowboys and the miners with whom to some extent they overlapped; and their songs of the tough life they led, especially those composed by Joe Hill, who was executed after being convicted of murder in 1915, belong now to the tradition of American folklore. Nevertheless these characteristics did not save the I.W.W. from condemnation and persecution as "un-American" during the First World War and afterward.

With the pressure of the Socialists and the I.W.W. on one side, and the attacks of the militant employers upon the other,

Trusts, Socialists, and Wobblies

it is not surprising that the A.F. of L. went more deeply into politics than ever before in this period. It was not that Gompers and his colleagues favored the establishment of an independent labor party; that issue was a dead one for them since the 1894 A.F. of L. convention, and no evidence in the form of successes by local labor parties had become available to cause them to change their minds. Nor did Gompers become any more favorable to Socialism as the Socialist movement increased in size; his tendency was rather to a more dogmatic opposition, as was illustrated by his declaration in 1903:

I want to tell you Socialists that I have studied your philosophy; read your works upon economics, and not the meanest of them; studied your standard works, both in English and in German— have not only read, but studied them. . . . And I want to say that I am not only at variance with your doctrines, but with your philosophy. Economically, you are unsound; socially, you are wrong; industrially, you are an impossibility.

But Gompers could not ignore the challenge to the status of the unions which was posed by injunctions and the outlawing of the boycott. The success of the British Labour Representation Committee early in 1906 in establishing a parliamentary Labour party of some thirty members also had its influence upon him. Accordingly, in March, 1906, he and other A.F. of L. leaders drafted a Bill of Grievances which they submitted to President Roosevelt and to Congress and in which they demanded, among other things, legislation against the use of injunctions and action to establish the eight-hour day for government employees. When this received a cool reception from Republican leaders, Gompers and his colleagues decided to take a vigorous part in the 1906 election campaign, in order to "stand by our friends and administer a stinging rebuke to men or parties who are either indifferent, negligent, or hostile." A special Labor Representation Committee was appointed to take charge of the campaign, and Gompers himself went off to agitate in the district of Congressman Littlefield of Maine, whom he regarded as particularly hostile to labor. But the campaign bore little fruit. Gompers was not successful in unseating Congressman Littlefield; and although the Republican majority in the House was substantially reduced, labor interests did not seem to benefit.

Then, in 1908, came the Bucks' Stove injunction and the decision in the Danbury Hatters case, and also a Supreme Court ruling invalidating an important section of the Erdman Act of 1898, which had illegalized discrimination against union members on the railroads. A presidential election was at hand, and Gompers prepared the ground carefully for an indorsement of the Democratic party by the A.F. of L. First he initiated a new "Protest to Congress," which as he expected received scant attention from the Republican majority. Then he submitted the program of the A.F. of L. to both the Republican and Democratic national conventions. The Democrats showed themselves much more friendly to its contents, and Gompers was able to give them his emphatic indorsement. The bulk of the union leaders accepted Gompers' lead, although a few supported the Republicans, the Mine Workers took up an attitude of neutrality, and some unions, mostly locals, indorsed the Socialist candidate, Debs.

The willingness of the membership of the A.F. of L. to accept Gompers' support of the Democrats sprang from a number of causes. One of them was the careful public preparation of the official decision, by means of the "Protest to Congress" and the approach to both national conventions. Another was the willingness of Democratic politicians, who had been out of office for some time, to take the initiative in seeking labor support and to offer pledges on future legislation. A further not unconnected reason was the large number of normally Democratic voters who were to be found in the ranks of the A.F. of L. The Democratic party catered much more than the Republicans did to first and second generation immigrants, especially those of them who were Catholics; and it has been maintained that a numerical majority of the members of the A.F. of L. were Catholics at this time. Catholic influence in the A.F. of L. was also a factor in limiting the Socialists to a minority role in its proceedings. For the time being, however, the A.F. of L. indorsement of the Democrats seemed to make little difference; the Republicans again won the presidency and also both Houses of Congress. The A.F. of L. was hampered in its intervention, not only by the limited extent of its membership as compared with the total electorate, but also by its own traditions of internal autonomy and abstention from politics, which had become deeply ingrained in the preceding twenty years.

In 1909 and 1910, however, the temper of the country began to change. The Republican party itself was divided owing to the emergence of a strong Progressive movement in its ranks; and at the 1910 elections the Democrats were naturally the beneficiaries, winning control of the House. William B. Wilson, a former secretary-treasurer of the Mine Workers, who represented a congressional district in Pennsylvania, became chairman of the House Labor Committee. In 1911 and 1912 bitter dissension went on inside the Republican party, and in the end former President Roosevelt emerged as the presidential candidate of a new party, the Progressives. This virtually insured the success of the Democratic candidate, Woodrow Wilson; so that although the A.F of L. went

through the motions of putting its program to all three major
national conventions, and although Roosevelt's supporters gave
an even more favorable reply than Wilson's, there was no
question of the A.F. of L. failing to support the Democrats
in this election. Wilson had an easy victory, with Roosevelt
running second; and the Democrats were in control of both
Houses of Congress.

President Wilson was the first American President to pay
serious attention to the advice of the leaders of organized
labor. He frequently discussed matters personally with Gompers, and one of his first acts was to create a separate Department of Labor, with William B. Wilson as its first secretary.
Congress, too, began to pass legislation favorable to labor interests. The most important act at the time seemed to be the
Clayton Act, passed in 1914, which declared that "The labor
of a human being is not a commodity or article of commerce,"
and specified that unions were not to be regarded as illegal
combinations or conspiracies in restraint of trade, as they had
almost come to be regarded under the terms of the Sherman
Act. The Clayton Act also appeared to narrow the use of
injunctions in strikes. But a decision of the Supreme Court
in 1921 would show that all these clauses had made little real
change in the law, and that a secondary boycott was still
illegal, even if it was only a matter of a national union giving
assistance to one of its locals. Nevertheless, when the Act
was passed, its grandiloquent language suggested that it was
a great advance, and Gompers hailed it with enthusiasm as
the "Magna Carta" of labor.

By this time the tide of public opinion was flowing strongly
in favor of unionism. Apart from the generally liberal and
progressive mood of these years, events during the Colorado

coal strike of 1913–14 gave rise to criticism of the behavior of employers in industrial disputes. In April, 1914, a tent colony of striking miners was set on fire by state militia, causing the death of two women and eleven children. The President made repeated efforts to secure an end to this strike, but his overtures were rejected by the company, although welcomed by the miners. It was in this atmosphere that the Commission on Industrial Relations, authorized by Congress after the McNamara case, held the bulk of its deliberations. The result was a series of public hearings and a final report which were bitterly hostile to the corporations and very favorable to organized labor. A further important legislative achievement of these years was the La Follette Seamen's Act of 1915, which had been framed on the advice of Andrew Furuseth of the Seamen's Union. This Act limited the penalties that could be exacted from seamen under contract, drew up safety regulations for their life at sea, and guaranteed certain minimum standards of life aboard ship.

Whatever the apparent successes of the leaders of organized labor at the national level, however, it could not be said that they did very much to alleviate the lot of the less fortunate workers, other than the seamen. As had always been the case, there was a staggering gulf between the way of life of the best-paid and the worst-paid manual workers. At the top were the "aristocrats" of labor, the railroad engineers and conductors, the glass blowers, and some of the steel-mill employees and members of the building trades. These men earned anything from $1,500 to $2,000 a year—a very good wage at the existing level of prices. At the bottom were those adult male workers, numbering between one-fourth and one-third of the total employed in factories and mines, who were paid less than $10.00 a week; and also the majority of women workers engaged in industry or trade, who received less than $6.00 a week. In view of the fact that $700 a year was regarded as the minimum on which a family could be brought up without serious hardship, it was not surprising that statistics showed that in the larger cities from 12 to 20 per cent of all children were "noticeably underfed and undernourished."

There was also a wide range in the length of the working day and week, with the poorer and less well-organized workers generally having the worst of it. The shortest hours were in the building industry, where forty to forty-eight hours was now the usual weekly total. The cigar makers did roughly as well. Steelworkers on the other hand worked a twelve-hour shift, and the sixty-hour week was characteristic of meat packing. In coal mining there were many different arrangements, and it is not easy to generalize. Other trades mostly worked long hours, although the general tendency was for a reduction in this period, from about sixty hours in 1900 to more like fifty in 1917. Longer hours than this, however, were common in the South, in agriculture and domestic work, and also in the sweatshops of the larger cities.

It would not be true, of course, to say that the American workers as a whole failed to better themselves in this period. Real wages were, as we have seen, fairly constant; but the people receiving the lower wages and also working the longer hours were the new immigrants. All the same, owing to the absence of effective state and national supervision, conditions of work were allowed in the United States that would not have been tolerated in other industrial countries. This was partly because the workers who suffered most were usually immigrants, who could make little protest and rarely possessed the vote. It was also, however, because of the variety of legislatures concerned in the remedy of their ills and the ambiguity about their respective powers. In 1895 the Illinois Supreme Court declared unconstitutional a law restricting the hours of women workers to eight; and in 1905 the United States Supreme Court invalidated the ten-hour law for bakers in New York.

All this was disappointing enough; but it also became apparent in this period that the conservative craft unions were more of a hindrance than a help to the new immigrants in their difficult struggle for self-improvement. We have already seen that the less-skilled textile workers felt neglected by the A.F. of L. union in their trade; and this was also true of other trades. In the men's clothing industry, for instance, there was an A.F. of L. union, the United Garment Workers, founded in 1891, which had organized a fair proportion of specialized native workers but was unwilling to sanction strikes to extend its membership among the unskilled immigrants. In 1910 a spontaneous revolt of Jewish workers in Chicago substantially increased the size of the union, but the new recruits were restive, and in 1914 the friction between them and the old leadership led to the formation of a new union, the Amalgamated Clothing Workers, under the leadership of the young Sidney Hillman. Because the United Garment Workers held the original jurisdiction from the A.F. of L., Gompers could not grant a charter to the new union, and he felt obliged to force the United Hebrew Trades of New York, which was affiliated to the A.F. of L., to expel those Clothing Workers' locals which belonged to it.

In the women's clothing industry, the situation was not so bad, for the International Ladies' Garment Workers' Union, which had secured an A.F. of L. charter in 1900, was itself run by Jewish immigrants. But the lack of any substantial central organizing fund prevented Gompers from being able to do much to help this union in its early struggles. Its rapid advance in 1909–10, which began with the strike of New York needlewomen known as "The Uprising of the Twenty Thousand," was largely a spontaneous affair in which the most conspicuous outside help came from a society of middle-class sympathizers known as the Women's Trade Union League, and from various Jewish organizations.

Gompers himself was not oblivious to the need for an adequate national strike fund, to be at the disposal of himself and the executive council for the common benefit of all the unions. He had proposed such a scheme in the early days of the A.F. of L., but, as we have seen, he had failed to win approval for it. He tried again in 1914, supporting a proposal to empower the executive council to build up a fund financed by per capita contributions, for the purpose of providing assistance to national unions involved in strikes or lockouts. The proposal was defeated, its principal supporters among the unions being the three main industrial organizations, the Brewery Workers, the Mine Workers and the Western Federation of Miners (which had reaffiliated in 1911), and also the International Ladies' Garment Workers, the unhappy Amalgamated Association of Iron, Steel, and Tin Workers, which still needed all the help it could get, and the Hod Carriers, a union of laborers in the building trades. These unions probably contained the great bulk of the first-generation immigrants who belonged to the A.F. of L., but they were not powerful enough to win the day against the bulk of the craft unions on behalf of their as yet unorganized fellow immigrants.

Trusts, Socialists, and Wobblies

Equally serious was the fact that the A.F. of L., instead of supporting and pressing for every possible type of remedial legislation, chose either to oppose or to ignore many current proposals. In 1914 the annual convention declared against the eight-hour day by legislative action, except for women and children and government workers. Gompers himself also opposed both compulsory health insurance and unemployment insurance, and although schemes for both purposes were in operation in various European countries, the A.F. of L. took no action to bring them before the American public. Gompers explained his attitude by saying that national insurance was "at variance with our concept of voluntary institutions and of freedom for individuals," and presumably he felt that it would weaken the authority of the unions over their members, for in many cases they provided sickness and unemployment benefits.

Nevertheless, the early years of the twentieth century, and especially the ten years before the outbreak of World War I, saw a remarkable development of protective legislation for the benefit of the industrial worker. This legislation was enacted in all the states. Although the South remained more backward in most respects than the North, and the rural states were slower as a rule to act than those with a large industrial population, the general progress was remarkably uniform. This in itself suggests that it was the result of the advance of public knowledge and the general social conscience, rather than the work of particular political pressure groups.

A good example of the action taken as a result of information and public concern is provided by child labor legislation. The Industrial Commission at the turn of the century had noted the inadequacy of existing laws, particularly in the

South. But thereafter, the improvement was rapid. In 1903 no less than eleven states, including five in the South, enacted child labor laws. In 1904 a National Child Labor Committee came into existence to press for still more progress and uniformity between the states. The laws unfortunately did not extend as a rule to agricultural work and domestic service; and there was a good deal of ambiguity about how far state laws were effective, and how far federal action would be constitutional. In 1916 a federal child labor law was enacted to cover all those who had any part in the production or distribution of goods which passed through interstate channels, but two years later this was declared unconstitutional by the Supreme Court. The question of child labor was also closely bound up with that of school attendance. In 1900 only seven states had laws for compulsory school attendance up to the age of sixteen, but by 1915 the number of states with such legislation had increased to thirty-three.

Other forms of industrial legislation received their greatest impetus in the heyday of the Progressive movement, from about 1908 onward. The Pittsburgh Survey, a careful social study of a key industrial area in 1907–8, produced much evidence of overwork and distress. The Women's Trade Union League and the National Consumers' League were active in pressing for the restriction of women's hours; and although legislation had at first been delayed by doubts about its validity, a favorable decision of the United States Supreme Court in 1908 over the Oregon law launched a flood of enactment on the subject. Between 1908 and 1917 no less than nineteen states, and also the District of Columbia, limited women's hours by law for the first time, while another twenty states improved their existing laws.

Trusts, Socialists, and Wobblies

Industrial managements, especially those of the larger corporations, took the lead in efforts to reduce the danger of industrial accidents. The U.S. Steel Corporation took advantage of its enormous size to pool information about the causes of accidents and to provide advice on how they might be avoided. The Chicago and North Western Railroad set an example to the other railroad companies by establishing safety committees composed of officials and workers. The American Institute of Social Sciences and the Association of Iron and Steel Engineers both took up the question of industrial safety, and in 1916 a National Council for Industrial Safety was organized. In the "sweated trades," a good deal of impetus was given to the movement by a disastrous fire at the Triangle Waist Company in New York City in 1911 which caused the loss of 145 lives. A New York Factory Investigating Commission was appointed, and it revealed that the system of factory inspection was completely inadequate. The enactment of laws for workmen's compensation in various states from 1910 onward was also of great importance, as it gave employers a powerful economic incentive to improve the conditions of industrial safety.

At the outset of World War I the industrial codes of the various states still varied widely, but nearly all of them were very much advanced by comparison with 1900. In 1911 the state of Wisconsin, under the control of the La Follette Progressives, had set up an Industrial Commission with executive, quasi-legislative, and quasi-judicial functions to secure the safety and health of industrial workers. Other states soon followed this lead, and in 1912 Massachusetts set up a Minimum Wage Board with authority to determine the minimum legal wage for any occupation—but without authority to secure enforcement. The general minimum wage question, incidentally, was one which found the American Federation of Labor ranged on the side of the employers. According to the report of the executive council of that body in 1913: "If it were proposed in this country to vest authority in any tribunal to fix by law wages for men, Labor would protest by every means in its power."

In the early years of the twentieth century the conditions of American labor seemed to have changed considerably from those which had originally made them unique in the world. The urban industrial class was now very large, and its members were rarely able to contemplate escaping from the grimy environment of the city to the peace and comparative security of a farming life. There were many people now who doubted whether the lot of the American worker could possibly be happier than that of his European counterpart. The propaganda of the Socialists, the muckrakers, and other critics of American society suggested the contrary.

And yet, the immigration continued. Most, it is true, came from the poorest countries of Europe, and many of the immigrants were escaping from persecution. But even Edwardian England, for all its social legislation, continued to send a proportion of its working class to the United States. The Mosely Commission of visiting British trade unionists in 1902 were impressed by the better conditions of work in American factories; and the percipient H. G. Wells, visiting New York a few years later, spoke of its "exceptional prosperity" by comparison with London. "Even in the congested entrances, the filthy back streets of the East Side," said Wells, "I find myself saying as a thing remarkable, 'These people have money to spend.' "

Furthermore, the immigrants had a faith in the promise as well as in the immediate reality of American life. Political freedom, good educational facilities, and the continuous expansion of the economy insured that their children and grandchildren would be able to improve their social and economic status. Only the Negro seemed not to be in a position to benefit from this continuous process of advancement. The white Americans, and the newcomers from Europe, were busily climbing a stairway of betterment, and the prospect even from the bottom steps seemed not uninviting. The variety of conditions of the manual worker in America, implying as it did a variety of opportunity, remained as before a characteristic of a society otherwise much altered by the growth of industrialism and urbanization.

VI

Suffering from Prosperity

The participation of the United States in the actual hostilities of World War I was comparatively brief—nineteen months —but even before American intervention the war had great influence on the country's economic life. The demands of the Allies for munitions and other supplies created a trading boom in 1915–16 which wiped out the existing unemployment. At the same time, immigration halted abruptly, cut off by the lack of Atlantic transportation, and the extra labor that northern industry began to need could only be provided by internal migration, notably by the movement of Negroes from the South. Heavy demand for goods, coupled with full employment, resulted in a rapid rise of prices. Manufactures rose in price by 98.4 per cent in the period 1913–18, and the general cost of living went up by 77 per cent in about the same period.

The end of the war did not result in any immediate collapse of this boom. The unfulfilled demands of consumers kept industry busy in spite of the cancellation of war contracts; and

Suffering from Prosperity

for a time there were continued orders from the Allied countries, which were starting their reconstruction. Manufacturing prices continued to rise steeply; by 1920 they were 139.5 per cent above the 1913 level. Strikes were numerous as the workers strove to keep wages at a level comparable to or higher than that achieved during the war. In this they were successful, but not much more than that: in 1920 wages on the average were in money terms 118 per cent above the 1914 level, but in real terms they were only 6 per cent higher.

The collapse of the postwar boom took place in 1920. By this time, foreign orders were falling off and domestic unfulfilled demand was largely at an end. Agricultural prices soon fell to approximately prewar figures. Prices of industrial goods, which could be controlled more readily by cuts in production, did not fall so rapidly. But unemployment mounted swiftly to 4.5 million, and wages were cut heavily—although those still at work were on balance able to benefit from the even greater fall in prices.

This sharp deflation in 1920–21 turned out to be the prelude to a more stable period of development. Demand for agricultural produce did not recover, and farming remained depressed throughout the decade, the actual numbers employed in agriculture no longer increasing as they had in the past. In 1919 farmers received 16 per cent of the national income, in 1929 only 8.8 per cent. But industry in general went ahead with rapid strides, the secondary and service trades especially. The output of manufactures increased by 64 per cent in 1919–29, while the labor force actually declined. This was made possible by improved methods and by the application of new techniques of management, such as the assembly line and "time and motion study" based on the ideas of Frederick W. Taylor and others. The use of new sources of power, especially petroleum and natural gas, expanded rapidly; and new industries mushroomed into prominence, the most remarkable being the manufacture of automobiles. By 1929 the automobile industry itself was the largest single manufacturing industry, employing half a million workers; but in addition it was estimated that in one way or another the use of automobiles gave employment to 3,700,000 persons. The manufacture of radios, of electrical products generally and of aircraft also grew with great speed.

Undoubtedly this rapid development of new industries helped to keep competition alive and to counterbalance the trend to monopoly which still characterized individual industries. It also provided a stimulus for the economy as a whole at a time when slackness might have been expected owing to a decline in the rate of population growth. Unrestricted immigration had come to an end with the enactment of strict legislation in 1921 and again in 1924; and the natural increase was also slowing down. Much of the increase of population which did take place between 1920 and 1930—16.5 million, bringing the total to 123 million—was due to an improvement in the nation's health rather than to more births.

The absence of a substantial flow of new immigrants, forming a reserve of cheap labor, accounts in part for the rapid rise of real earnings of the average American worker in the 1920's. This amounted to 26 per cent, probably the largest decennial increase up to that time. It provided a sharp stimulus to the service trades; a building boom took place, and the market for consumers' goods underwent a great expansion, assisted by the extension of credit facilities. By 1929 automobile registrations numbered more than 23 million; by 1930 two of every five families had radio sets, and weekly attendances at motion picture theaters averaged about 115 million. Already by 1929, however, the boom was becoming highly unstable. Stock exchange prices far exceeded the prospects of income from the shares, owing to a fever of speculation which infected even a proportion of the wage earners.

The inevitable and yet unexpected collapse took place in October, 1929. The panic depressed business but did not directly occasion the years of slump that followed. The process of causation was more intricate; it involved the whole structure of international trade, which in the 1920's had come to depend upon American overseas investment. When the panic caused the cessation of that investment, European finances began to go wrong, and in 1931 the dislocation of world trade became acute. The European collapse which followed reacted on the American economy, turning a depression of not unusual dimensions into a unique catastrophe. Employment, which by January, 1931, had already fallen to 70 per cent of the 1929 level, declined still further to only 50 per cent in late 1932; and even this figure concealed a great deal of underemployment. Prices fell rapidly, and cuts in wages kept pace with them, so that the worker lucky enough to remain in full employment did not on the average suffer a loss of real income. But all around him misery and destitution stalked the land, unalleviated by any national system of unemployment insurance. Although President Hoover had in 1932 initiated a policy of credit expansion and public works, it was not surprising that his administration did not survive the elections of that year, and his rival for the presidency, Franklin D. Roosevelt, was elected in his place.

Already in August, 1916, over seven months before the United States declared war, President Wilson had shown his desire for the co-operation of organized labor in case of need. He then invited Gompers to join the seven-man advisory council of the Council of National Defense, and to take the chairmanship of the Council's Committee on Labor. Gompers himself, by accepting the appointment, guaranteed the A.F. of L.'s willingness to co-operate with the President —a matter of great importance at a time when both the Socialist movement and the I.W.W. were hostile to American intervention under all possible circumstances. In March, 1917, when the declaration of war was imminent, a conference of officers of the national unions of the A.F. of L. met in Washington and pledged their assistance to the administration, demanding in return the right of "representation on all agencies determining and administering policies of national defense."

After the American entry into hostilities, a rapid development of such agencies took place, and organized labor secured its representation on those which directly concerned labor conditions and wages. A Cantonment Adjustment Commission was set up by the War Department to insure that standards accepted by the unions were enforced in the work of building the new army camps. On it were represented the army, the public, and organized labor. Similar bodies were later created for other types of contracting by the army, for shipbuilding, and for the arsenals and navy yards. A series of strikes which broke out in the West, affecting the supply of important strategic materials such as copper and lumber, led to the appointment by the President of a special Mediation Commission, which settled many disputes itself and reported on the causes of the others. The I.W.W. had been active in several of the strikes, but the Commission found more fundamental causes of unrest in the autocratic behavior of many western employers. In August, 1917, a Labor Adjustment Commission, consisting of representatives of management, labor, and the public, was set up to settle disputes which the normal processes of mediation and conciliation under the Department of Labor had failed to settle. With the assumption of public control over the railroads in December, 1917, it became necessary to create a special Board of Railroad Wages and Conditions.

All this administrative and quasi-judicial machinery—only the barest outline of which has here been drawn—caused a substantial improvement in the working conditions of a large part of the labor force. Government contracts had to be fulfilled under conditions approved by the unions in the appropriate trades; in many occupations wages rose rapidly, and workers for the first time received the freedom to join trade unions without the danger of being discriminated against as a result. Conditions of work, according to the policy of the federal government, were to correspond as closely as possible to the best peacetime standards. For women who worked on government contracts, the principle of "equal pay for equal work," which had been demanded by the A.F. of L., was conceded, and both hours and conditions of work were carefully supervised. The variety of good jobs available at slightly different rates of pay encouraged a tendency on the part of many workers to move quickly from job to job; and by the end of 1917 it became clear that there was an urgent need for a co-ordination of the government's labor policy, not only to insure some equalization of rates of pay and conditions, but also to eliminate wasteful competition for labor between different departments and government contractors.

In 1918 this co-ordination was largely achieved by a series

of administrative reforms. A National War Labor Board was set up to act virtually as a supreme court for labor disputes. In point of fact, it had no powers of enforcement, but the President used his war powers to secure obedience to its decisions—threatening recalcitrant workers with the draft and in one or two cases overcoming the opposition of managements by commandeering their plants. A War Labor Policies Board was set up under the Department of Labor to co-ordinate the labor policies of all government departments concerned; and the recruitment of all unskilled labor for government work was channeled through the local offices of the Department of Labor's Employment Service.

Generally speaking, American workers supported the war, and the opposition, such as it was, was ethnic and ideological rather than on a basis of social class. The Socialist Party of America, which maintained its attitude of neutrality to the world conflict, rapidly lost popularity with the industrial workers; its most steadfast supporters were those with strong ethnic ties to neutral or hostile countries, and this very fact made it vulnerable to charges of disloyalty. It was the I.W.W., however, which could most effectively interfere with the war effort by encouraging wartime strikes. As we have seen, it had some success at first, but this was largely through the exploitation of bad conditions, which the government's labor policies could and did put right. Although strikes were more numerous in 1917 than in 1916, in 1918 they dropped to a figure lower than in either of the two preceding years. Gompers and his leading colleagues were encouraged by President Wilson to rally the flagging spirits of the workers in the allied countries of Europe. This task they undertook with enthusiasm, but with only limited success, as they insisted on denouncing Socialism wherever they went, whereas most of the European labor leaders, whether enthusiastic or not for the prosecution of the war, were friendly toward Socialism.

The freedom to organize was a great boon to the unions. Membership rose rapidly from 2,800,000 in 1916 to over 4,000,-000 in 1919, the A.F. of L. proportion being at least three-quarters of the total. Among those workers who joined unions in the largest numbers during the war and immediately afterward were the seamen, the longshoremen, meatpackers, and machinists. Railroad employment, which was directly under government control, became one of the most highly organized of all occupations; large gains were made among the clerical staff and the shop crafts, while the brotherhoods of the operating crafts came to include almost all who were eligible for membership.

One feature of the period was a considerable movement of Negro labor from the South to meet the need for unskilled workers in the industrial centers. Over four hundred thousand, it has been estimated, went north to work in the Pittsburgh and Calumet steel mills, in the Chicago stockyards, and in the automobile plants of Detroit. Always they had difficulty in finding housing, and in spite of the general shortage of jobs, their entry into new employments was often hotly resented by white workers—especially when, as in the Chicago stockyards, it seemed to be a deliberate move by the management to prevent unionization. For the fact was that Negroes were usually either entirely ignorant of unionism or, as a result of bitter experience, downright hostile to it. In July, 1917, a serious race riot took place at East St. Louis, where Negroes had been imported to break a strike at the Aluminum Ore Company. In 1918, with the general improvement in the gov-

ernment supervision of conditions of work and the recruitment of workers, such incidents were avoided.

The end of the war saw a speedy end to most of the gov-
ernmental controls affecting labor. The U.S. Employment Service was used to place many of the returning veterans in jobs,
but it soon expired for lack of congressional appropriation.
Price control was ended, and owing to the pressure of unfulfilled demand, prices rose faster than in wartime. The result
was a whole crop of strikes as the unions sought both to safeguard their position as bargaining agents and to keep wage-
levels in line with prices. Early 1919 saw two sensational developments: a general strike at Seattle, which soon broke
down after an impressive display of workers' solidarity; and
a policemen's strike at Boston, which was suppressed with
severity by Calvin Coolidge, then governor of Massachusetts.
The Amalgamated Clothing Workers won a strike for the
forty-four-hour week, and the textile workers won the eight-
hour day. Dockers, longshoremen, telephone operators, and
railway workers also safeguarded their positions in various
ways by strike actions. The total strength of the unions rose
to over five million in 1920, of which four million were
affiliated with the A.F. of L.

But these successes were not quite as impressive as they
seemed. Even at five million, the union membership still
amounted to only about one-eighth of the total working population, and only about one-fifth of the wage-earners. Moreover, many of the new recruits to unionism had been won
in wartime, under the protection of the government. What
would happen when a depression came along, under peacetime circumstances, with managements anxious to return once
more to non-union conditions? This question could not as

yet be answered. In the steel industry, however, it had already become clear that a determined anti-union management had strong cards to play. In the fall of 1918, no less than twenty-four unions with some element of jurisdiction in the steel industry had banded together to form the National Committee for the Organizing of the Iron and Steel Industry. The leaders of this body were William Z. Foster, a radical who had been a successful organizer in the meatpacking industry, and John Fitzpatrick, the president of the Chicago Federation of Labor. After a year's preparation, they launched a strike in September, 1919. By January, 1920, however, the strike had failed completely, partly because of the use of Negro strikebreakers, partly because of public hostility to some of the radicals associated with the strike, but also in no small part simply because there were twenty-four jurisdictions involved, which placed serious restrictions both on the resources of the organizing committee and on its power to organize effectively. In spite of their five million members, therefore, the union leaders had reason to reconsider their tactics very carefully for the ensuing era.

In 1920 Gompers attained his seventieth birthday, but he showed no sign of willingness to retire from his onerous responsibilities as president of the A.F. of L., which he had held (with one year's break) for thirty-four years. Gompers enjoyed many aspects of his work: a self-important little man, inclined to overdo his respectability of appearance as if he were a mortician, he liked to feel that he and no one else could speak for "Labor" and, by so doing, carry weight in the counsels of the nation. As Grand Chief Warren S. Stone of the Locomotive Engineers rather unkindly put it, "Sam likes to be in the limelight and likes to be played up. . . . In fact if he were going to walk around the block, he would want to be preceded by a brass band."

It was inevitable that after the war, in which Gompers had been afforded a position of such importance by President Wilson himself, he should carry ever greater prestige among his fellow unionists. Although we do not know the full details of discussions on the executive council, it seems that now more than ever Gompers could persuade his colleagues to follow his lead. But his influence was rarely thrown on the side of innovation in policy. He believed, as before, that the way to success for the unions lay through securing the respect of employers and managers and through avoiding the toils of state intervention.

One new departure Gompers did encourage, but that was in general conformity with the other aspects of his policy. He made explicit his approval of "scientific management," the new technique of improving the efficiency of the worker by time-study and by carefully planned wage incentives. When the pioneer of "scientific management," Frederick W. Taylor, had first advocated his system a generation earlier, he had coupled it with a rigid hostility to the recognition of collective bargaining, and the unions had naturally opposed its introduction. But Taylor had died in 1915, and a new generation of efficiency experts had arisen who showed a much greater willingness to associate their schemes with recognition of the unions. Gompers now recognized that the movement had come to stay and that the unions would be obliged to accept it sooner or later. He also realized that a voluntary acceptance would not only win wage increases for union members but would put the unions at a premium with at least some managements because they would be co-operating in the task of overcoming the natural hostility of the workers to the new procedure. It is not altogether clear how far Gompers succeeded in carrying the craft unions with him in this change of policy. But at least it was put into effect in the machine shops of the Baltimore and Ohio Railroad, and later copied elsewhere.

In spite of the advantages that the unions had gained from the conditions of wartime state control, Gompers reverted to an attitude of thoroughgoing opposition to welfare legislation, let alone state ownership of industry. In 1920 his views on compulsory health insurance were indorsed by an A.F. of L. committee, which reported that it "would lead to the control of a great many of the activities of the organizations of labor that now are unhampered by state or other interference." Unemployment insurance he opposed for the same reason; if it were introduced, "the labor movement would lose its voluntary character and its effectiveness." It was indeed an acknowledgment of the absence of militant class consciousness among the American workers, or at least among the organized workers, that Gompers should imagine that their interest in unionism would be seriously threatened if some of the union benefit functions were supplemented by the state.

There were, however, some critics of various aspects of the philosophy of "voluntarism." First of all, and rather surprisingly, there were the railroad brotherhoods. The brotherhoods had by no means lost all their earlier characteristics of extreme conservatism, and indeed the Locomotive Engineers had enhanced them by using their surplus funds to establish banks and investment trusts and even to operate a non-union coal mine. But their experience of wartime federal control of the railroads had been so much to their liking that they wished to perpetuate it, and so they adopted a scheme of nationalization known as the "Plumb Plan." The federal government's powers over interstate commerce would have enabled Congress to enact the plan into law; and in order to increase their lobbying strength, the brotherhoods in 1919 applied for membership in the A.F. of L., assuming that this would win them the co-operation of the larger part of organized labor. Gompers and his colleagues, however, appear to have been alarmed by this sudden desertion of laissez-faire principles on the part of the brotherhoods; and they drew out the negotiations for affiliation, raising various issues of competing jurisdiction with unions already chartered. Against the opposition of Gompers himself, the 1920 A.F. of L. convention indorsed the Plumb Plan; but the brotherhoods were meanwhile making a compromise with the railroad companies to safeguard their wartime gains, and so lost interest either in enacting the Plumb Plan or in joining the A.F. of L.

Among the A.F. of L. unions, the opposition to Gompers' leadership was led by the United Mine Workers, the largest of the industrial unions, which succeeded in pledging the A.F. of L. convention to the nationalization of the mines. It might be supposed that after the failure of the 1919 steel strike the Mine Workers would be able to mobilize a strong movement in favor of transforming the policies of the executive council. But as the unions grew older, so their leaders tended to become professionalized and to lose interest in the salvation of the entire working class. In any case the political left was in a state of disintegration, partly owing to the divisions caused by the Russian Revolution and partly as a result of the prosecutions initiated by Attorney General Palmer in 1919–20.

Suffering from Prosperity

In 1921 the new president of the Mine Workers, John L. Lewis (who was no radical himself) stood against Gompers as a candidate for the presidency of the A.F. of L.—the first challenge to Gompers' leadership since the candidacy of Max Hayes, a Socialist, in 1912. He secured 12,324 votes against Gompers' 25,022, and this minority was a very assorted coalition of persons who were for one reason or another disgruntled with the existing leadership—not only were dedicated industrial unionists and Socialists included, but also groups of craft-union leaders, like those of the Brotherhood of Carpenters. After this trial of strength, the challenge to Gompers' leadership was not renewed at subsequent conventions.

Meanwhile the unions had been thrown on the defensive by a renewed employers' open-shop campaign, comparable to that organized at the beginning of the century. The concept of the open shop was dubbed the "American Plan," implying that opposition to it was somehow un-American and meant being associated with foreign creeds like Bolshevism. This was an effective propaganda move at a time when passions were roused against the Communist threat of world revolution. The fact that Gompers had been an almost fanatical opponent of Communism since its emergence in 1917, and that A.F. of L. conventions had invariably supported his denunciations of it, made little difference. Under the weight of the campaign, the unions rapidly lost ground, especially those which had made the greatest gains during the war, such as the Railway Clerks, the Seamen's Union, the Amalgamated Meatcutters (which had been strong in the packing industry), and the unions in the metal trades.

The courts seemed to reflect the same anti-union trend. Successive decisions of the U.S. Supreme Court weakened the power of the unions. In 1921 *Duplex* v. *Deering* showed how limited were the possibilities of legal boycott under the Clayton Act, and *American Steel Foundries* v. *Tri-City Trades and Labor Council* closely circumscribed the limits of peaceful picketing. In 1922 injunctions were again being freely granted against striking unions, and in the Coronado case the Supreme Court held that unions were suable and their funds liable for damages in cases of tort arising from strikes. Injunctions were also based upon the use of the "yellow dog" contract, which forced employees to promise not to join a union or go on strike. Such contracts had existed before (usually under the name of "ironclad" contracts) but not on so wide a scale.

It is not to be wondered at, therefore, that the A.F. of L. was pressed to make the most of its strength in the political sphere. Its four million members ought to have been able to carry much more weight at the polls than the two million members of prewar days—at least if they could persuade their wives to vote with them for candidates favored by their leaders. The strongest pressure for a militant political policy came from the Chicago Federation of Labor, which under the strong personality of John Fitzpatrick pressed for the formation of a Labor party, like that of Britain. Gompers opposed the idea and, in the course of the early 1920's, steadily whittled away the constitutional rights of the city federations inside the A.F. of L., realizing that they were no longer so important in relation to the national unions as they had once been.

Gompers adhered to his political policy of "rewarding labor's friends and punishing its enemies," which he had carried out before the war; but, in view of the conservatism of both major parties on questions affecting labor, it was with little enthusiasm that he faced the elections of the early 1920's. In 1924 there was a revival of the Progressive movement, and a coalition of groups, Socialist and liberal, and representing both farmers and industrial workers, formed a body called the Conference for Progressive Political Action and nominated Senator Robert M. La Follette as their candidate for the presidency. Having lost its earlier influence in the Democratic party, the A.F. of L. decided to support La Follette; and this could be done the more easily because the Progressive party did not put forward any supporting ticket of congressional candidates. La Follette secured almost five million votes, and did well in the northern cities; but he carried only his home state of Wisconsin. Labor's power at the polls had not been demonstrated very convincingly.

At the end of 1924, it seemed clear that the A.F. of L. was sorely in need of a more vigorous leadership. In the preceding four years, the membership had dropped by about 1,200,-000—30 per cent of the 1920 total. Yet the principal obstacle to change seemed now to be Gompers himself, and he, though ailing, was unchallengeable; indeed the 1924 convention was the quietest on record, with hardly any debate taking place and not a single roll-call vote. All of a sudden, however, the obstacle disappeared: shortly after this 1924 convention, Gompers died at the age of seventy-four. William Green, secretary-treasurer of the United Mine Workers, who was known to be a critic of some of the extremes of "voluntarism," was elected by the executive council to succeed him as president. Here at last, it seemed, might be the beginning of a new era.

The five years starting in 1925 were years of prosperity for the American people as a whole—years in which unionism might have been expected, on the basis of past experience, to make rapid headway. This, however, did not happen. The membership of the A.F. of L. remained almost stationary, at a little less than three million. This meant, in fact, that it was not even keeping up its proportion of the total labor force, which was growing by more than half a million every year.

To blame William Green for this failure is perhaps unfair. Certainly, expectations had risen at the time of his election. But those who knew him best realized that he was not likely to be as strong a leader as Gompers—and it was indeed for this reason that the craft unions had favored his elevation to the presidency; he was to be a prince among peers, and not, as Gompers came to be at the end of his life, a monarch among men. Green was not a fighting man; he believed in the powers of persuasion, backed by facts and figures. His colleagues on the executive council knew that he would not bully them. In their minds, the principle of craft autonomy remained the guide to action—or inaction—inside the A.F. of L.

The feeble attempts of the A.F. of L. to "organize the unorganized" in this period illustrated the situation only too well. In 1926, for instance, Green initiated a conference of unions with jurisdictional claims in the automobile industry, and he pointed out in his address that the only way to conduct an organizing campaign was to suspend these jurisdictional claims, at least temporarily. Several of the unions refused to agree to this proposal; and those which did, and continued to support the organizing campaign, provided so little in the way of funds and other assistance that the campaign sputtered out within a few months. This was in spite of the fact that the unions were richer than they had ever been before and were following the lead of the Locomotive Engineers in founding banks and setting up investment trusts and the like in order to find a home for their surplus of revenue. The

William Green (*left*) presents an A.F. of L. Charter to the president of the American Federation of Government Employees, 1932. (Acme.)

Leaders of the C.I.O. Left to right (*front*): Philip Murray, John L. Lewis, Sidney Hillman. (Courtesy, AFL-CIO News.)

Sit-down strikers at the Fisher Automobile plant, Flint, Michigan, 1937. (Acme.)

Pickets in action during a strike at the International Harvester plant, Chicago, 1952. (Courtesy, Chicago Historical Society.)

campaign was in any case never a militant one, because Green had recurring hopes that one or another of the employers would consent voluntarily to unionism.

Another opportunity for extending the bounds of unionism was presented by the growth of industry in the South. For some time the textile industry had been developing rapidly in various southern towns, partly because of the availability of cheap labor there and partly because of the favorable tax status of new industry in the southern states. In 1929 a number of spontaneous strikes took place in mills in North and South Carolina, in Virginia, and in Tennessee. President Green sent in several A.F. of L. organizers and raised a certain sum of money for a campaign in the mills; but little permanent success was achieved. Many of the strikers were black-listed and some were evicted from their homes. Yet the A.F. of L. convention of 1929 was sufficiently aroused to order a general organizing campaign in the South, not just restricted to textiles. The national unions were asked to contribute both money and organizing help. But little help was in fact forthcoming, and the campaign failed in part for want of resources. Another reason for failure was the fact that once again Green could not make up his mind whether to adopt militant tactics or to try to persuade the employers by friendly discussion that collective bargaining was a good thing. The growth of unemployment in the course of 1930 naturally provided another important reason for the collapse of the campaign, which had come several years too late.

It is easy enough to see why unionism was forced on the defensive in the years of depression that were to follow. But why had it proved so unsuccessful in a period of unusual prosperity? One factor, undoubtedly, was the skill of management

in providing substitutes for many of the advantages of unionism. Large firms undertook the practice of securing employee
representation by plant councils or shop committees, and a
considerable proportion of the industrial labor force—over 1.5
million by 1928—were organized in this way in "company
unions." The system was especially widespread in the metal
trades, where the tide of independent unionism which had
risen so rapidly during the war had ebbed with equal speed
in the early 1920's. Various means were also found to develop
the individual worker's loyalty to his employer, so that he
would be unwilling to risk losing his job by engaging in union
activities. For instance, schemes of profit sharing were initiated,
and company stock was sometimes offered on attractive terms.
Employee insurance and pensions, usually forfeited if the
worker left the employment prematurely, clearly had a similar
effect. There was also a great extension of welfare facilities
such as company housing, sports clubs, hospitals, cafeterias,
house magazines, and so on. Many of these techniques were
derived from the experience of wartime, and it would be
wrong to assume that they all had the ulterior purpose of
preventing independent unionism. But in association with
the general improvement of wages and the reduction of the
standard working week resulting from the immense increases
in productivity in these years, they served to discourage many
of the unorganized workers from seeking the assistance of
the unions.

Other reasons for the failure of the unions were to be found
in their own changing character. Many of them had once
been militant organizations in which most of the organizing
was done on a voluntary basis, with democratic systems of
control and a general atmosphere of fellowship and enthu-

siasm. Some of them were still of the same character, but, in general, increasing size and age eliminated these factors. For the sake of efficiency, it had long become necessary for the larger unions to place a great deal of power in the hands of full-time officials; and full-time officials, especially in craft unions, were less likely to be interested in general concepts of working-class solidarity than were the volunteers whom they replaced. Furthermore, as time went on not a few of them succumbed to the temptation of feathering their own nests at the expense of the members of their unions. This last step could of course only be taken in unions where the systems of democratic control were no longer functioning effectively.

Various forms of graft had developed in the building trades, which were among the first to be organized, as early as the turn of the century. The "walking delegate," or full-time organizer employed by the local, often had plenary powers to call strikes, and it was easy for him to extort handsome sums from employers at times when they had urgent work on hand. Not far behind the building trades were the teamsters, especially those of Chicago, who at the moment of forming a national union in their trade had already developed a collusive contract with the local coal team owners' association. Under the terms of the contract, non-members of the association were unable to operate because they could not obtain labor.

Corrupt practices of this type owed their existence to the weakness of class solidarity among the workers and to the absence of effective law enforcement systems in many cities. Their greatest development took place in industries of a highly competetive character, where numerous small employers were fighting hard to gain advantages over one another. In the

1920's a new dimension was added to the problem with the general growth of racketeering, often associated with violence. In the New York clothing trades, for instance, gangsters and hoodlums were used by both employers and local unions in the attempt to control labor relations; and the leadership of national organizations such as the Amalgamated Clothing Workers and the Ladies' Garment Workers had to make strong efforts in order to prevent large sections of their unions from being completely dominated by these sinister influences. In some trades, gangsters found it to their advantage to form their own fictitious "locals" in order to practice extortion at the expense of businessmen.

Under these circumstances, the unorganized workers tended to lose sympathy with unionism; and the union officials, whether honest or not, for their part rarely developed a missionary zeal to extend the boundaries of unionism, unless such extension was of immediate advantage to themselves. They guarded their jurisdictions jealously, but were unwilling to help their brothers in other organizations except on a strictly business basis. The slogans of class solidarity were now being repeated only by a small and disunited minority of Socialists and Communists. The Socialists endeavored to remedy the situation by educating the workers in their principles, as for instance at Brookwood College, an adult residential school to which unions were encouraged to send their members; the Communists controlled a body called the Trade Union Educational League, which had the highly practical purpose of winning control of the unions by "boring from within" and which was beginning to make some headway when in 1928 the word came from Moscow that "boring from within" was no longer the policy of the Communist International. It is doubtful, however, whether even a united and skilfully organized left wing (a concept difficult to conceive of under existing American conditions) could have attained very much success inside the A.F. of L., in view of the character of the leadership and the way in which it had by now intrenched itself in most unions.

In 1929 began the crippling sickness of the nation's economy which was to last for a decade. The distress of the years 1929–33 reached staggering proportions, and this was partly because of the initial failure to realize the depth of the economic crisis or to assess at any one time the actual extent of unemployment. The A.F. of L. performed a valuable service by publishing records of the proportion of its members who were out of work; but as its members were mostly skilled workers, who suffered less than the labor force as a whole, the figures underestimated the situation although they showed the major trends. Partly as a result of pressure from the A.F. of L., a count of unemployed persons was made at the time of the decennial census in March, 1930. It amounted to about three million, which was serious but not yet catastrophic. Unfortunately, the numbers continued to grow at a steady rate up to the end of 1932, when a total at least four times as large was reached. The proportion was highest in the construction and durable goods industries; it affected the unskilled more than the skilled; it was more acute among Negroes than among whites and among the young than among the more established workers.

If the lack of adequate statistics was one hindrance to a full appreciation of the problem, another was provided by the laissez-faire conceptions of the time, which encouraged a reliance upon the resources of private enterprise and private charity. Setting his face against the use of federal funds for relief or public works, President Hoover at first attempted to overcome the crisis by encouraging optimism in business circles; and this resulted in concealment of evidence indicating an increasingly serious situation. After all, the bread lines were not very conspicuous even in the large cities, and many people could easily be led to believe that not much was wrong. By the winter of 1930–31, however, it was becoming obvious that the various charity organizations were inadequate to deal with the numbers seeking relief. This was due at least in part to the overlapping of different agencies, which were co-ordinated only with considerable difficulty; but it was also due more and more to the sheer size of the demand for aid. In spite of constant fresh appeals, the funds of all agencies were rapidly reaching the point of exhaustion. The cities financed relief programs of their own and many of the industrial states did likewise, but here again, the money soon began to run out.

The most fortunate of the unemployed were probably those who were engaged on local public works; but this was only a small and decreasing minority, for it was felt that public works were considerably more expensive than the distribution of subsistence allowances or "dole." The latter, if it kept its recipients above the line of starvation, rarely made any allowance for clothing, rent, or other necessities such as medical treatment. Families were forced to share apartments with others or to move to vacant lots or to the outskirts of town, where they could improvise dwellings out of packing cases and sheet iron. These shanty towns were derisively known as "Hoovervilles." As the funds for relief ran out, starvation

threatened many. In Paterson, New Jersey, nearly all the unemployed were without relief of any kind. In Dallas, Texas,
it was denied to all Negroes and Mexicans. In Omaha, Nebraska,
all relief was discontinued owing to lack of funds.

In view of the desperate plight of so many people, careful
observers feared serious acts of violence or perhaps the emergence of a definite revolutionary impulse. Neither contingency
was realized. Here and there some act of carelessness or incompetence in the administration of relief occasioned rioting,
but there were rarely any fatalities. Some were drawn into
the agitation of the Communist party, which organized hunger
marches and other demonstrations. These however were hardly
ever on a large scale. The most remarkable demonstration was
one not run by the Communists—the "bonus army" which
assembled at Washington in the summer of 1932 to demand
the payment of veterans' bonuses. Altogether some fifteen
thousand men, mostly veterans themselves, convened at the
capital, and many of them established a shanty settlement on
the Anacostia Flats near the Potomac, whence they were driven
away on the President's orders by troops under the command
of General Douglas MacArthur.

By the summer of 1932, however, it was obvious that the
situation would get out of control if the federal government
did not act to support the relief programs of the states and
cities. So far, Hoover had refused to consider direct federal
assistance for relief, although he had secured the enactment
of a program of support for the farmers, and by the creation
of the Reconstruction Finance Corporation in January, 1932,
he had obtained powers to provide federal loans for banks and
other businesses threatened by collapse. Hoover's theory was
that this federal aid, given generously and in secret to ailing

enterprises, would seep down to the "little men" and the workers, providing them with employment in the end. But by 1932, these measures were too indirect to tide the country over an immediate crisis. The President therefore at last accepted the need for direct federal assistance to the states for emergency relief, and the powers of the Reconstruction Finance Corporation were expanded accordingly to enable it to act as the instrument of this purpose.

But to do Hoover justice, there were few who had a much clearer idea of what was needed to end the depression. His opponent at the presidential election of 1932, Franklin D. Roosevelt, throughout his campaign continued to urge the need for a balanced budget. As for organized labor, it was only in the summer of 1932 that the A.F. of L. abandoned its principle of "voluntarism" so far as to advocate the introduction of a system of compulsory unemployment insurance. As late as January, 1932, President Green had spoken of it as a "union-wrecking measure." The A.F. of L. fought hard to prevent wage cuts, realizing that their effect was to create a downward spiral of economic activity; and it also favored public works, apparently however without any perception of their value in "pump-priming" the economy. Nor was there much enlightenment to be obtained in academic circles —the Keynesian revolution in economic thought still lay in the future.

The labor unions suffered as they always did in a depression, although they had gained little in the preceding boom, for the unemployed, or the partially employed, could not afford to keep up their dues. A.F. of L. official membership totals dropped from about 3,000,000 in 1930 to 2,500,000 in 1932 and 2,100,000 in 1933. The real situation may have been still worse, for the Mine Workers, who claimed 300,000 members, probably really had only about half that number. The union had lost heavily owing to loss of demand for coal, mechanization of the pits, competition from the non-union coalfields of West Virginia, Kentucky, and the South, and the emergence of serious factionalism and "dual unionism" among the workers. Similarly, the Brotherhood of Railway Carmen, which had been seriously weakened by mechanization in the industry and also by the hostility of the railroad companies, was reporting a membership of 80,000, which was probably about twice its effective strength. All in all, by 1933 the A.F. of L. and the unions generally were representing a smaller proportion of the American population than they had since the depression of the 1890's.

In the late 1920's visitors to America, including many European Socialist leaders, marveled at the high-wage economy of the country, at the spectacle of unions collaborating with management in the introduction of efficiency methods, at the rapid expansion of productivity and of general prosperity. By the early 1930's, however, this happy picture had vanished; and immigrants were packing their bags to return to their native lands, in the expectation that state welfare schemes in Europe would look after them better than they had fared in the "land of opportunity." Such were the contrasts of these years.

Yet the depression in some ways only served to underscore the distinctions between American labor and that in other parts of the world. Lacking class consciousness, the American workers had allowed their leaders to formulate a policy of "voluntarism," which was closely akin to laissez faire, and which abhorred all compulsory welfare schemes for the adult males eligible to join the unions. This policy inevitably left the workers defenseless in time of economic depression, dependent on charity and lacking even the simple guarantee of a minimal regular "dole." In effect, the workers had gambled on the success of capitalism. While the system continued to make headway, there was a share of the profits for them; but when it failed, they lost their entire livelihood, but not their hopes and, indeed, expectations of the return of prosperity. This accounted for the failure of the Socialists and Communists to make much headway in the depression years. The "bonus army" was not Socialist or Communist at all, and for every man who joined its ranks, there must have been a hundred who preferred to roam the country in the traditional search for a better life by internal migration.

As for the leaders of the labor unions, they had accepted the economic system in its existing form quite as much as the workers as a whole had done. They had taken to investing their funds in the foundation of banks and in the purchase of real estate for speculative purposes; nearly all the banks had failed, and the real estate had become almost worthless. They had difficulty in formulating new policies to deal with the problems of the depression; and when opportunity knocked on their door in the 1930's, few of them were able to respond to the call. Nothing, in fact, could call the A.F. of L. leadership back to vigorous activity except the direct competition of rival organizations. If the awakening was bitter, it was because the slumber of the years had been long and deep.

Roosevelt and John L. Lewis

The period 1933 to 1945—from the year of Franklin Roosevelt's inauguration to that of his death—saw a truly remarkable transformation in the economic circumstances of most Americans. In 1933 the depression was at its deepest, and at the beginning of the year thirteen million workers were looking for jobs, the great bulk of them being dependent on public assistance or charity. The remainder of the decade was a period of slow recovery, never reaching full prosperity and with intermissions of increased unemployment. The early years of the European war, however, saw an increased demand for munitions and supplies, both for beleaguered Britain and for the United States defense forces. And then after the sudden jolt of Pearl Harbor the wartime condition of overfull employment set in and lasted until 1945. Thus although many of the measures of the Roosevelt administration and of Congress had an influence in cutting down unemployment, the sobering fact remains that it was only the onset of war which really restored the country to full prosperity in this period.

This lack of buoyancy of the American economy may be accounted for in a number of ways. Roosevelt himself attached some importance to the disappearance of the frontier, and it is true of course that the old type of expansionist boom based upon the settlement of new areas had now been lost. But there were other factors. The virtual termination of immigration and the decline in the birth rate meant that the population rose by only 7.2 per cent in the 1930's, which was only one-third the rate at the beginning of the century. To some extent the decline in the birth rate was itself due to poverty and unemployment, but the tendency had already been marked in the 1920's. Only in the 1940's was the trend clearly reversed when, with the additional advantage of some rise in immigration, the rate of population increase rose to 14.5 per cent for the decade.

But the slowing-down of population growth is by no means an adequate explanation of the absence of prosperity. After all, in the existing population there was a vast pent-up demand for consumer goods. There is no escaping the conclusion that the economy of the country, even under the stimulus of the New Deal, was not functioning satisfactorily. The explanation must be found in the fact that the measures of the administration were contradictory in their effect—that is to say, both restrictive and expansionist at the same time. This applied especially to the period of the "First New Deal," 1933–35, when restriction of output was pursued as a deliberate goal and the administration refused to co-operate with foreign countries in measures to rebuild international trading relations.

The principal domestic measure of this "First New Deal" was the National Industrial Recovery Act of 1933, under which

Roosevelt and John L. Lewis

the National Recovery Administration was set up. The object of this body was to stabilize industry by the evolution of a system which would guarantee fair price and wage levels and a reduction of hours. To secure this object, codes were to be drawn up for each industry, to which all employers were expected to adhere. The evolution of the codes had gone some way when in 1935 the whole structure was declared unconstitutional by the Supreme Court. Meanwhile, the immediate needs of the unemployed had compelled Roosevelt to institute various measures of relief and public works. The Public Works Administration, set up by the same Act as the National Recovery Administration, got going only slowly under the cautious control of Harold L. Ickes; but the Civil Works Administration under Harry Hopkins found immediate work for over four million in the winter of 1933–34, and the Federal Emergency Relief Act helped to sustain the relief programs of the states and cities.

In 1935 the President was obliged to start again. The N.R.A. had been declared unconstitutional, and in any case it had become clearer that the need was for expansion rather than restriction of the economy. The Works Progress Administration set up in May was authorized to find employment for up to five million unemployed, although in fact this figure was never reached. Other programs of an expansionist character were instituted to deal with agricultural resettlement, housing, and youth employment. The cumulative effect was to stimulate a marked recovery in 1936–37, and as a result it was decided to reduce substantially the number engaged in public works. Unfortunately, the recovery turned into slump once more, and in 1937–38 the total of unemployment rose again to ten million. The hasty re-employment of men on public works restored the partial recovery, however, and unemployment in 1939 was less than nine million.

The year 1940 saw a new stimulus to the American economy from British and French purchases of raw materials and (after the passing of the Pittman Act) of armaments on a "cash and carry" basis. The collapse of France caused an increase in these orders, although they were for Britain alone now, and also markedly stepped up the tempo of American defense preparations. Early in 1941 Roosevelt, now elected for a third term, sponsored the Lend-Lease Act which enabled Britain and then also Russia to call more readily upon American resources. The actual outbreak of hostilities for the United States as a result of the bombing of Pearl Harbor therefore found substantial sections of the economy, especially the armament industries, already going at full blast.

The new needs of industry in wartime and of the rapidly enlarged armed forces were met by an expansion of the total labor force to 65 million in 1944, as compared with 55 million in 1940. The armed forces took 15 million of these; but partly owing to the existence of unemployment before the war, the number of men actually employed in industry dropped by only four hundred thousand from the 1940 figure of just over 28 million. The new demands were met to a considerable extent by the increased employment of women, whose numbers rose from 11 million to 17 million. In certain occupations it proved necessary for the administration to restrict the freedom of workers to change their jobs; but the positive direction of labor was never resorted to.

Domestic consumption was kept in check by increased taxation, and prices were to some extent held down by various controls under the Office of Price Administration. Compared with the 1939 level, by 1944 wages in manufacturing had risen by about 25 per cent in real terms, if reckoned on the basis of hourly earnings; but by about twice as much, if the payment for extra hours worked is added in. The strain on the economy imposed by these gains and by the upward movement of profits and salaries would not have been so easily sustained if there had not been a simultaneous vast increase of the gross national product, by at least 50 per cent from the beginning of the war. Thus the United States was able to send large expeditionary forces to all quarters of the globe, to furnish a substantial proportion of the equipment of its allies, and still to maintain a standard of domestic consumption not substantially different from that of peacetime.

Although the inauguration of President Roosevelt in March, 1933, is usually regarded as the beginning of a new phase of labor history, it is important to bear in mind that congressional legislation had already taken a new turn as a result of the 1930 elections, which returned majorities in both Houses opposed to the Hoover administration. Although the A.F. of L. had played little part in any election since 1924, in 1932 Congress passed a measure very favorable to the interests of organized labor—the Norris–La Guardia Act. This Act restricted the power of the federal courts to issue injunctions against unions engaged in peaceful strikes; and it also made "yellow dog" contracts unenforceable in the federal courts. These were important gains for labor, but they were overshadowed by what was to come, with the great Democratic landslide of the 1932 elections.

The first piece of legislation sponsored by the new President which affected the position of organized labor was the National

Industrial Recovery Act. Section 7(a) of this Act declared that workers had "a right to organize and bargain collectively through representatives of their own choosing," and specifically forbade any "interference, restraint or coercion" by employers in this process of choosing representatives. The A.F. of L. leaders had had some influence on the phrasing of this section, which enormously improved their prospects of "organizing the unorganized." It also owed a good deal to precedents of war-time control and to the Railway Labor Act of 1926, by which the railroad brotherhoods had secured important guarantees of their own rights. Other parts of the Act affecting labor—particularly the arrangements for the fixing of minimum wages under the industrial codes—were opposed by the A.F. of L., which at least in this respect had not abandoned its sacred principle of "voluntarism" even in the depth of the depression.

Of the immense benefit of section 7(a) to the labor movement there could be no doubt, provided that the Act was enforceable. It was not only that the Supreme Court had yet to pass on its general validity; there was also a lack of machinery for enforcing the workers' right to choose their own bargaining representatives without interference by hostile employers. In fact, the passing of the Act was followed by a large increase in company unions, which were clearly established with the purpose of preventing the growth of the independent unions. In August, 1933, the President set up a National Labor Board under the chairmanship of Senator Robert F. Wagner to settle differences between employers and employees which arose owing to the Act; and in February, 1934, this Board was authorized to hold elections of employees to choose their bargaining representatives. Later in the same year the system was changed by a Public Resolution, sponsored by Senator Wagner, which authorized the President to create a National Labor

Relations Board to conduct elections and to hear disputes. But it was still impossible to enforce its decisions against recalcitrant employers.

Early in 1935, therefore, Senator Wagner introduced new proposals for legislation which, owing to the invalidation of the N.R.A. codes, proved acceptable to the President and were passed with his support as the National Labor Relations Act—more commonly known by its sponsor's name as the Wagner Act. This not only reaffirmed the principle of section 7(a) of the National Industrial Recovery Act, but also made permanent provision for a three-man National Labor Relations Board (N.L.R.B. as it became known) to hold elections for the purpose of determining bargaining agents and also to insure that employers should not indulge in "unfair labor practices." These practices were defined to include not only discrimination against individual employees but also the domination of or interference with a labor organization and the refusal to bargain collectively with the legal representatives of the employees. Decisions of the Board were made enforceable through the federal circuit courts of appeals.

Although precedents could be found for many of the provisions of the Act, either in the practice of wartime or in railway legislation, the novelty of the statute as a whole was its favorable treatment of the unions by comparison with the employers, for the unions suffered no restrictions whatsoever and were even free to bargain for and to secure the closed shop. At the same time, it ran the risk of invalidation by the Supreme Court, just as earlier legislation had done, if the Court should retain its limited interpretation of the powers of Congress. It therefore did not come into full effect until the Supreme Court had passed favorably on it in April, 1937.

Meanwhile the tide of reform which the depression had set

moving was still in full flood. The states were passing more social legislation than they had passed since before the war. Minimum wage laws for women and children were enacted by several states, and hours legislation was generally extended. The most effective pressure for these changes came from the National Consumers' League and from the Women's Trade Union League, rather than from the A.F. of L., while the Department of Labor, by providing expert assistance, also played an important part. Roosevelt had acted wisely in appointing a social worker, Miss Frances Perkins, rather than a senior official of the A.F. of L. as his Secretary of Labor, for she at least had no inhibitions about the desirability of legislative action. It is true, however, that the A.F. of L. did belatedly change its policy on a number of issues of social welfare: for instance, it accepted the desirability of compulsory unemployment insurance in 1932, by which date only one state, Wisconsin, had yet enacted legislation on the subject. The question was taken up by Congress in 1934 in the Wagner-Lewis bill, which included an ingenious device for encouraging state legislation and co-ordination on the subject.

Later in 1934 the President proposed action on both unemployment and old age insurance, and a joint measure took shape in 1935 as the Social Security Act. At one bound a vast system of social welfare came into existence, although the need for co-ordination with the states and validation by the Supreme Court prevented benefits being available in many cases until the end of the decade. In the preparation and enactment of these schemes, the A.F. of L. had little contribution to make. It had no research staff to deal with the complicated problems concerned, and moreover its enthusiasm for the legislation was very lukewarm, as was apparent at its 1935 convention.

Roosevelt and John L. Lewis

To complete the story of major New Deal legislation, it should be added that in 1937, after the Supreme Court had moved to a more generous interpretation of the interstate commerce power in accepting the constitutionality of the Wagner Act, the President urged the passage of legislation establishing a minimum wage and a maximum working week for all workers. This resulted in the enactment of the Fair Labor Standards Act, the principle of which was strongly opposed by certain A.F. of L. leaders, in particular William L. Hutcheson, the president of the United Brotherhood of Carpenters. As a consequence President Green of the A.F. of L. was obliged to take a highly equivocal attitude toward the bill during its passage. But in spite of this labor opposition, which undoubtedly resulted in some watering-down of its provisions, it was passed into law in 1938 and proved of value in raising the standards of a certain number of poorly paid workers.

How far did the organizing efforts of the A.F. of L. make up for its hesitations in the political sphere? Certainly its member-unions were not slow to take advantage of the favorable atmosphere engendered first by the National Industrial Recovery Act and then by the Wagner Act. As early as 1933 the industrial unions made considerable headway: the United Mine Workers at last won back West Virginia, where for many years non-unionsm had been the rule; the International Ladies' Garment Workers quadrupled its membership in 1933–34; and the Amalgamated Clothing Workers (which affiliated with the A.F. of L. in 1933) did almost as well. Many other unions improved their position, though less spectacularly; and the executive council of the A.F. of L. again authorized special organizing campaigns in the mass-production industries. These campaigns, however, somehow never got under way. Some progress was made in the auto industry, but it was clear that the workers did not like the arrangements that the A.F. of L. made for them. They were recruited into federal labor unions of the A.F. of L., which were not autonomous but paid substantial dues to the executive council; and they were given to understand that in due course those of them who were skilled workers would be parceled out among the various craft unions which claimed jurisdiction in the industry. The same was true both in steel and in the rubber industry. The result was that in each of these industries successful organizing was not possible, and the recruits who were secured tended to lapse from membership within a few months. By the end of 1934 there was little to show for what campaigning the A.F. of L. had done.

These failures led to bitter conflict within the A.F. of L. leadership over how the campaigns should be managed. At the 1934 convention a compromise resolution between opposing points of view was carefully worked out and unanimously approved; but this solved nothing, and a year later the situation in the mass-production industries had not improved. Nothing effective had been done in steel, and although charters had been given for national unions in the auto and rubber industries, in neither case were they comprehensive charters, and the workers had not responded with enthusiasm. The 1935 A.F. of L. convention was riven by dissension when the resolutions committee split eight to seven on the question of how to deal with the problem. The majority took the view that it was necessary to safeguard craft jurisdictions at all costs; the minority favored abandoning them in the mass production industries, so as to mobilize the workers on an industrial basis. In spite of eloquent speeches by the minority and the bitter scorn of John L. Lewis, their principal spokesmen, who derided the organization of the workers into "fifty-seven varieties" of crafts, the majority position was indorsed by the convention by 18,204 votes to 10,933. Two-thirds of the minority vote came from the Mine Workers and the Clothing Workers. At a later stage in the convention, Lewis and Hutcheson of the Carpenters exchanged sharp words, and Lewis struck Hutcheson on the jaw—an act that symbolized the rift in the organization.

After the convention was over, the minority leaders established a Committee for Industrial Organization (C.I.O.), with Lewis as chairman. In forming this body they claimed to be acting within their rights as members of the A.F. of L. But the executive council, realizing that they would soon be trespassing on the chartered territory of other unions, at once demanded the disbanding of the committee. The rebels remained obdurate, and they were joined by the new unions founded by the A.F. of L. in the auto and rubber industries, as well as by the Amalgamated Association of Iron, Steel, and Tin Workers. On complaint from various of its affiliates, the A.F. of L. executive council in August, 1936, found the unions belonging to the C.I.O. to be guilty of "dual unionism" and gave them one month in which to withdraw from the C.I.O. or be suspended from the A.F. of L. The C.I.O. unions did not respond to the ultimatum and were accordingly suspended. At this point, the American labor movement was effectively split in two.

The immediate cause of the split was obvious enough: the conflict of craft jurisdiction with the needs of mass industry, where craft counted less and occupational proximity was more important. Yet the hostility of the craft unions to a loss of jurisdiction inevitably reflected the peculiar character of the American labor movement, in which class solidarity is weak and ethnic or racial differences have tended to heighten feeling between the skilled and the unskilled. At the same time, it is difficult to believe that the split would have taken place if Green had been a more powerful president of the A.F. of L., or if Lewis had been a less ambitious rival. Certainly, by 1937, when the C.I.O. had proved its point by its success in organizing, the case for reunion was strong, and the feeling for it both in the A.F. of L. and in the C.I.O. was warm. There is little doubt that if at that time Lewis had been willing to reach agreement, agreement could have been reached. But Lewis had tasted the pleasures of national leadership, and he was not prepared to take a subordinate role once more, so the negotiations collapsed.

If Lewis' personal vanity was a disadvantage for the labor movement, his sense of drama was important for the success of the C.I.O.'s organizing drive. He realized that if money was to be spent, it must be spent in a big way. He displayed this characteristic most conspicuously in the summer of 1936, when he offered Roosevelt $500,000 from the Mine Workers' treasury for his second presidential campaign. This grandiose gesture was for Lewis a business investment. He expected Roosevelt to treat him as his labor adviser in his second term, and to do as he was advised. Roosevelt did not regard the gift in this light, however, although he was grateful for the money, which was of great assistance in his campaign. The Amalgamated Clothing Workers and the International Ladies' Garment Workers also contributed liberally, and the total union contributions to the campaign came to over $770,000—a staggering sum when compared with the $95,000 which represented the total contributions of the A.F. of L. executive to national political campaigns in the preceding thirty years.

It is true that the C.I.O. unions could do little effective local campaiging in 1936, except in New York where the American Labor party came into existence as a convenient medium for their activity. Both A.F. of L. and C.I.O. leaders were represented in a national body called Labor's Non-Partisan League, which supported Roosevelt, but it is doubtful if it had much influence. At any rate, the enthusiasm for Roosevelt's re-election was so strong among the workers as a whole that it needed little special organizing; and Roosevelt was re-elected with the record number of 523 electoral college votes to 8 for his Republican opponent, Alfred M. Landon.

Meanwhile, Lewis and his colleagues were also engaged in industrial organizing; and the same instinct for the big gesture was apparent in their financing of organizing campaigns, which were backed by sums of the order of half a million dollars, instead of the few thousands that the A.F. of L. had been able to allot from its meager central treasury. As it turned out, the money was being spent at a most propitious time, for in the spring of 1937 the Supreme Court ruled favorably on the constitutionality of the Wagner Act, and this caused many employers to weaken or to abandon their previous hostility to collective bargaining.

Furthermore, a new and dramatic technique of striking had been developed in the mass-production industries: this was the "sit-down" strike, whereby the workers stayed in the plant where they worked, defying the company to expel them or to replace them with strikebreakers. The technique had been used in the rubber industry early in 1936, but it acquired its greatest publicity on the occasion of the auto workers' strike at the Flint works of General Motors in January, 1937. The police were unable to remove the strikers and Governor Murphy of Michigan refused to mobilize the state militia. Consequently, General Motors had to give way and recognize the union. A further "sit-down" strike against Chrysler in April had a similar conclusion. The result was that the auto industry became effectively organized except for Ford, and by the fall of 1937 the union could claim 400,000 members. But the "sit-down" strike did not survive as a union technique. It had had surprise value, but was clearly illegal, and was declared so by the Supreme Court. In any case it depended for its efficacy upon support by public opinion and the state authorities, which was not likely to continue.

Lewis' greatest concern, however, was with the steel industry, which employed many former coal miners, which owned a number of coal mines (the so-called "captive mines"), and which was now being tackled by a Steel Workers Organizing Committee appointed by Lewis and supplied by him with $500,000 from the Mine Workers' funds. Lewis' choice for the leadership of this body (which swallowed up the old and ineffective Amalgamated Association) was Philip Murray, for many years a vice-president of the Mine Workers. He and his colleagues gradually won over the company unions that had lately been set up in the industry. Then, early in 1937, the policy of the United States Steel Corporation rather unexpectedly changed, and after secret talks between Lewis and Myron Taylor, its chairman, the Steel Workers Organizing Committee was recognized as a bargaining agent by the Corporation's subsidiaries, and wage increases and a forty-hour week were conceded. This was Lewis' greatest success, though it owed not a little to the fortunate coincidence of a growing demand for steel output, adverse publicity for the employers derived from the La Follette Committee's inquiry into industrial espionage and violence, and the changing attitude of the Supreme Court on issues arising from federal legislation. As in the auto industry, however, the success of the union was not complete. The four companies of "Little Steel" refused to capitulate, and in the summer of 1937 they defeated a strike to organize their plants—a strike that lasted for several months and was marked by bloodshed, notably the "Memorial Day Massacre" at South Chicago when police killed ten strikers.

In other industries, too, the C.I.O. made rapid advances. In rubber, contracts were won from the firms at Akron, Ohio, where the industry is centered, and the membership of the United Rubber Workers rose above 70,000 in 1937. In textiles, the task was taken over by a Textile Workers Organizing Committee run by Sidney Hillman, whose union, the Amalgamated Clothing Workers, financed the operation with a contribution of $500,000. This campaign was not very successful, as many of the cotton mills were in the South, where resistance to unionism was still effective, being reinforced in some places by the Ku Klux Klan.

The C.I.O. also benefited by further secessions from the A.F. of L. and by the formation of other new unions. In March, 1937, all the unions forming the C.I.O. were formally expelled from the A.F. of L., with the exception of the International Ladies' Garment Workers; and in the fall of that year the C.I.O. held its first convention, and claimed a membership of 3,718,000—probably an inflated figure, but obviously a total to challenge that of the depleted A.F. of L. In 1938, recognizing the need for establishing itself on a more permanent basis, the Committee for Industrial Organization slightly changed its name and became the Congress of Industrial Organizations, retaining the initials C.I.O. The second convention accepted a constitution somewhat similar to that of the A.F. of L., except that it provided for the payment of considerably larger per capita taxes from the unions to the executive, in order to maintain the financing of large-scale national organizing campaigns. John L. Lewis became the first president of the C.I.O., with Philip Murray and Sidney Hillman as vice-presidents.

Meanwhile the A.F. of L. unions had also been sharing in the advantages of the Wagner Act, and—perhaps of even more importance—they recognized the threat to their existence posed by the progress of the C.I.O., and reacted accordingly. There was a revival of militancy and of enthusiasm for the recruitment of new members; and if on balance the A.F. of L. was not quite as militant as the C.I.O., this also could be turned to advantage, for many employers signed up voluntarily with A.F. of L. unions in order to avoid having to bargain with the C.I.O. Conflicts between A.F. of L. and C.I.O. unions of course became frequent, but many of them were dealt with by the N.L.R.B. through its electoral procedures, which proved to be a good way of preventing strikes if not of avoiding ill-feeling.

Although some of the A.F. of L. unions, such as those in the building trades, had comparatively little scope for rapid expansion, others increased their membership considerably. The Teamsters, for instance, aided by the growth of the trucking industry, rose in the 1930's from 95,500 to 350,000 and became the largest union in the A.F. of L. The Machinists expanded from 77,000 to 190,000 in the same period and virtually transformed itself into an industrial union of the type that its leaders had so strongly denounced in 1934 and 1935. The Hotel and Restaurant Workers, assisted by the ending of the

Roosevelt and John L. Lewis

Prohibition era, jumped from only 38,000 in 1929 to 185,000 a decade later. In some industries the potential union membership came to be divided between the A.F. of L. and the C.I.O. on a regional basis—for instance in the longshoring industry, the A.F. of L.'s International Longshoremen's Association dominated the Atlantic Coast, and the C.I.O. Longshoremen's Union controlled the Pacific ports. The A.F. of L. also had its share of newly founded unions, mostly rather small, and at least one substantial secession from a major C.I.O. industrial union—the United Auto Workers, A.F. of L.

All this meant a tremendous expansion of the total union membership. In 1938 this probably reached almost nine million, of whom about one million were in independent unions and the remainder were divided about equally between the A.F. of L. and the C.I.O. Even if we allow for some inflation of the figures, especially by the far from stable C.I.O. unions, this is still a staggering increase by comparison with 1933, when the total was less than three million.

With the outbreak of the European war in 1939, the political attitudes of union members and their leaders suddenly assumed special importance. The split in the labor movement inevitably prevented such united support for the policies of the administration as Gompers was able to pledge to Wilson in 1916, and to achieve in 1917–18. Furthermore, there were two major complications in the C.I.O., one at the highest level, the other at all lower levels of the union hierarchy. John L. Lewis had bitterly resented Roosevelt's failure to use him as his principal labor adviser, and he now took up an attitude of hostility to the President's international policies. At the same time, the Communist party, which had won control of a minority of the

C.I.O. unions and was influential in others, adopted a policy of complete neutrality from the date of the Nazi-Soviet Pact in August, 1939, until the invasion of Russia in June, 1941. The A.F. of L. and the bulk of the C.I.O. membership did however support the Roosevelt foreign policy.

The conflict inside the C.I.O. was especially conspicuous at the time of the presidential election of 1940. Lewis came out with an indorsement of Roosevelt's Republican opponent, Wendell Willkie, and in this he received the tacit support of the Communists, as well as the vocal approval of a certain isolationist element. But both Communism and isolationism were losing their former popularity; and Sidney Hillman, the spokesman of the strongly anti-Nazi Jewish unions, provided effective leadership for the Roosevelt forces inside the C.I.O. Lewis did all he could to make the members of the C.I.O. vote against Roosevelt, even declaring that he would resign from its leadership if Roosevelt was re-elected; but few, even of his own Mine Workers, followed his lead, and after Roosevelt's victory he was obliged to resign as he had promised. He was succeeded as president of the C.I.O. by Philip Murray, his former lieutenant in the Mine Workers who was now head of the Steel Workers Organizing Committee—and, incidentally, a supporter of Roosevelt.

Even before the election, however, Roosevelt had made his choice of a principal labor adviser for national defense. In the course of framing social legislation he had got to know and like Sidney Hillman, whom he found both intelligent and reliable. In October, 1940, he made Hillman a member of the National Defense Advisory Commission, with special responsibility for labor questions. A few months later Hillman was appointed associate director-general of the Office of Production Managament, which, under William Knudsen, was set up to organize the defense program. Needless to say, Hillman had to pay great attention to soothing the sensibilities of the A.F. of L., which had thus been deprived of the highest responsibility; but this was a task not unsuited to his abilities.

Already the contracts made by the British government and the mounting defense program of the United States itself had transformed the employment situation. Wage rates rose rapidly and prices also moved upward as demand increased. Much overtime was being worked, and women and older workers were drawn into employment. At first the supply of Negro labor was not adequately tapped, but in June, 1941, after a threat by A. Philip Randolph, president of the Brotherhood of Sleeping Car Porters (a Negro union), to organize a march on Washington, the President established a Committee on Fair Employment Practice. Thereafter, a migration of Negro workers from the South to the northern industrial cities began to develop as it had done during the First World War. The attitude of the unions was no longer as severe a bar to Negro advancement as it had been previously, for although many of the A.F. of L. unions and the major railroad brotherhoods continued to discriminate as before, the large C.I.O. unions including the Auto Workers and the Steel Workers had recruited Negroes from the start and became the champions of equal rights.

The unions were now industrially in a very strong position; but they had less support from public opinion than they had had during the New Deal period. The employers' organizations, especially the National Association of Manufacturers and the Chamber of Commerce of the United States, were active in anti-union propaganda, and engaged in strong criticism of the

operations of the N.L.R.B. In 1939 several states adopted legislation imposing restrictions on the unions to parallel those on
the employers; and after the Nazi-Soviet Pact of that year, disquiet began to grow about the influence of Communists in
the unions. In 1940 the public grew increasingly hostile to
strikes at a time of national danger and tended to blame the
unions for them, especially the Communist unions. In some
cases, such as that of a strike by a Communist-controlled local
of the United Auto Workers at Allis-Chalmers in Milwaukee,
there seemed to be a deliberate attempt to hinder the nation's
military preparations.

In order to keep strikes to a minimum, in March, 1941,
Roosevelt established a National Defense Mediation Board with
equal representation of management and labor. But this body
had no power to enforce its decisions, and few major strikes
owed their solution to its efforts. A stoppage at the Ford Plant
at River Rouge came to an early end when Henry Ford decided
voluntarily to recognize the United Auto Workers and also to
concede the union shop and the "check-off" (deduction of
union dues from the workers' pay envelope). Thus the last
major fortress of non-unionism in the auto industry collapsed.
The "Little Steel" companies also gave way, though less de-
cisively, under pressure from the N.L.R.B., and entered into
collective bargaining with the Steel Workers Organizing Committee. Then in June, when a Communist-led strike at Ingle-
wood, California, led to a cessation of work on aircraft manufacture, Roosevelt ordered the army in to enforce the continuity of production.

The Communists soon changed their policy on strikes when
the Germans invaded Russia; but John L. Lewis did not change
his. In April he had held the bituminous miners on strike for

a month; in September he called out the workers in the "captive mines," which directly supplied the steel industry. The latter event caused Roosevelt to speak harshly of "the selfish obstruction of a small but dangerous minority of labor leaders"; but it also caused the virtual collapse of the Defense Mediation Board because the C.I.O. representatives on it withdrew. The dispute was settled only by concessions awarded by a special three-man arbitration board which included Lewis himself. Thus at the end of 1941, although the unions were still making gains either by the threat of striking or by actually striking, each new advance made them more unpopular with the general public—a situation which could obviously lead to hostile congressional action. In fact, a bill to place drastic limitations on the unions had just passed the House of Representatives in December, 1941, when it was shelved as a result of the bombing of Pearl Harbor.

The immediate result of Pearl Harbor was a strong upsurge of patriotic feeling and a desire to abandon all internal disputes until the war was won. Taking advantage of this situation, Roosevelt secured a no-strike pledge from a conference of leaders of A.F. of L., C.I.O., and independent unions. In January he created a National War Labor Board to replace the old Defense Mediation Board; and this new body had the advantage of being able to call upon the President's wartime powers for the enforcement of its decisions. All the same, it had very difficult problems to face.

One of these problems was the pressure of the unions to secure the closed shop, or the union shop where they had not yet achieved it, as a means of maintaining a degree of security against both rival unions and non-unionism. The employers were much averse to conceding this advantage, and the public members of the board were uneasy about its element of compulsion on the individual. A compromise was however achieved by devising the formula of "maintenance of membership," whereby workers already unionized were obliged to remain in the same union or lose their jobs. In many decisions of the board the employers secured the provision of an "escape" period which allowed union members to leave the union if they so desired before the arrangements for "maintenance of membership" came into operation. But few union members ever made use of the "escape" provision. By 1945 about four million workers were employed under "maintenance of membership" conditions.

Equally difficult problems were presented by wage claims in wartime, for as time went on, the administration pressed more and more strongly for the limitation of wage demands in order to combat inflation. In the first months of wartime prices rose considerably, and the board felt obliged to concede wage increases in line with the rise in the cost of living. It also pursued a policy of raising substandard wages and eliminating anomalous differentials by wage increases. In the important "Little Steel" case of July, 1942, it worked out a formula for measuring what should be awarded, on the basis of increases in the price level as indicated by the Bureau of Labor Statistics Cost of Living Index. But this was too much for the administration, and later in the year, after the passage of the Stabilization Act, the President forbade the granting of wage increases which threatened the general price level. This caused the board to refuse wage increases beyond the "Little Steel" level, and in February, 1943, in the case of the workers in the "Big Four" meatpacking companies it rejected the wage demands altogether on the ground that the workers had already received increases in excess of this level. In April, 1943, the board's power to increase wages in particular cases in order to remove anomalies was taken away by executive order of the President, issued on advice of the Director of Economic Stabilization.

It was not surprising that this policy aroused discontent in the unions, for prices continued to rise, and in any case it could be argued that the Cost of Living Index used by the Bureau of Labor Statistics underestimated the real increase in the workers' actual costs. Many employers were in fact willing to pay much higher wages than the board allowed in disputes referred to it. As usual, the union leader who was most unwilling to accept this situation was John L. Lewis. In May, 1943, he threatened a strike, refusing to appear before the War Labor Board which he described as a "discredited political agency." Roosevelt took up his challenge and ordered government seizure of the mines; but he could not prevent the Mine Workers from coming out on strike. The upshot was a face-saving concession by Harold Ickes, on behalf of the government, whereby the Mine Workers were given substantial wage increases in the form of special allowances for travel time and a reduced lunch break.

A further crisis occurred on the railroads in December when the Director of Economic Stabilization vetoed a concession awarded to railroad employees under the Railway Labor Act. Here again the army was ordered to take control to prevent a strike before a compromise was worked out. No strikes of equal importance occurred in 1944, but unrest continued to grow, and by early 1945 one C.I.O. union, the Textile Workers Union, had formally announced that it was abandoning the no-strike pledge which its leaders made after Pearl Harbor.

In spite of all difficulties, the time lost in wartime strikes was remarkably small. It was proportionately less, for instance, than in Britain in the comparable period. Yet public opinion was aroused to great indignation by the major strikes that occurred, and particularly by the Mine Workers' strikes, which interfered directly with the war effort. In the heat of the moment Congress passed over Roosevelt's veto the clumsy and ill-contrived Smith-Connally Act, which laid heavy penalties on strikes in government-controlled works. The Act also ordered the taking of a ballot among union members before any strike could take place; and it placed restrictions on union political activities. All its provisions, however, applied only to the wartime emergency. The state legislatures, especially those of the southern and western states, also took action, passing acts restricting the unions and outlawing the closed shop. Thus although at the end of the war union membership reached the record level of 14,800,000, it looked as if the labor movement would have little chance to retain the favor of public opinion and the support of both Congress and administration that it had had in such full measure in the New Deal period.

Yet whatever the future attitude of public opinion, of Congress, and of the administration, there could be no doubting the astonishing transformation of the labor movement in the twelve years of the Roosevelt epoch. In 1933 the A.F. of L. had seemed to be little more than an "association of coffin societies" as its critics called it—a group of artisans' benefit societies run by old men whose only anxiety was to retain the friendship of management. Since then the C.I.O., based upon the mass production industries and run by young and militant leaders, had come into existence in a strength double that of the 1933 A.F. of L. It had also achieved the feat of reshaping the A.F. of L. almost in its own image—or, at least, of rejuvenating that body to an extent hardly conceivable in the early 1930's. In 1943, by an act of cynical realism, John L. Lewis admitted that there was no real difference of principle left between the two national centers; having taken his Mine Workers out of the C.I.O., he applied for readmission to the A.F. of L. His application would no doubt have been accepted had it not been for jurisdictional difficulties concerning his catch-all District 50; but because of that, his application was kept pending, and after a year he withdrew it.

What was it, then, that kept the A.F. of L. and the C.I.O. apart, once the intractable personality of Lewis had swept out of the C.I.O. leadership? Certainly Roosevelt did all he could to bring the two bodies together, realizing that the schism was both a national disadvantage and a political embarrassment to himself. But the jurisdictional tangle could not easily be sorted out, nor could the personal ill-feeling of the preceding few years readily be forgotten. The influence of the Communists in the C.I.O. was also a barrier to unity, both because they thought that unity would be a disadvantage to themselves and because the A.F. of L. leaders regarded them with the profoundest hostility.

Attitudes to national politics and to political action may provide the key to the problem. The C.I.O. as a whole continued to be much more radical than the A.F. of L., and although both bodies were united in support of Roosevelt in the 1944 election, they had different candidates for the vice-presidency. The C.I.O. favored the nomination of Henry A. Wallace, while the A.F. of L. was for Senator Harry S. Truman of Missouri. At the Democratic convention, Wallace could not command enough votes, and the C.I.O. then switched its support to Truman, who was at least acceptable to them. It was in the negotiations preceding this convention that Roosevelt is supposed to have made the remark "Clear it with Sidney," indicating the political influence of his labor adviser, Sidney Hillman. If the A.F. of L. and the C.I.O. were now agreed on their presidential ticket, there was nevertheless a good deal of difference in their respective efforts to elect the candidates. Carefully circumventing the provisions of the Smith-Connally Act, the C.I.O. formed a political action committee which worked hard for Roosevelt, basing itself during the actual campaign on individual contributions rather than on union funds. Altogether it spent some $1,328,000. Nothing at all comparable was done by the A.F. of L.

This greater political activity by the C.I.O., combined with its greater radicalism, is an indication of an important difference of outlook between the two bodies. Although by 1945 they were remarkably similar in structure, it was still true that the A.F. of L. retained something of its traditions of "voluntarism" and of limited political activity. The C.I.O. represented the new immigrants of the 1890's and afterward, who owed almost everything to politics: it had provided them with social legislation, with emergency relief, with opportunities to organize. The A.F. of L. had secured a lot from the same source, but not quite so much as that. As the years passed without further heavy immigration, these differences were bound to disappear; but they had not yet gone. They helped at this juncture to keep the labor movement divided, and to perpetuate the heterogeneity which we have frequently remarked upon in the course of our story.

VIII

From Taft-Hartley to Hoffa's Act

The late 1940's and the 1950's form the steadiest, if not the fastest, period of American economic development. This was probably due in large part to the high level of government expenditure, which tended to have a stabilizing effect upon the economy, limiting the effects of both booms and slumps in private business. Agricultural prices, guaranteed by federal supports, acquired unaccustomed steadiness; and social security benefits helped to maintain consumers' demand. But most of the increase in government expenditure was occasioned by the international situation. It consisted either of appropriations for the armed forces, for defense contracts and for military research, or of grants to assist foreign countries in their economic and military development. Naturally, the extent of these expenditures varied from time to time in accordance with the apparent urgency of the need. Immediately after the end of World War II, there were heavy cuts in both military expenditure and foreign aid. In 1947, however, the special program

for assistance to Greece and Turkey and the initiation of the
European Recovery Program (Marshall Plan) restored foreign
expenditure to a high level. The defense budget also began to
rise once more, and expanded rapidly three years later as a
result of the outbreak of the Korean War.

The emergency measures which were provoked by the
Communist invasion of South Korea in July, 1950, and particularly by the intervention of Chinese "volunteers" three
months later, caused some strain on the American economy,
which was reflected in a rise of prices. But the 1950's for the
most part provided an effective demonstration of the capacity
of the country to maintain a very high level of defense expenditure and foreign aid without hindrance of a continued
rise in domestic consumption. After the Korean War, the price
level at first fell back a little and thereafter rose only slowly.
The trade recessions of 1949, 1954, and 1958, although severe
in their impact on some industries, did not occasion more than
temporary rises in the over-all figures of unemployment, and
never to a level at all comparable with the lowest annual total
of the 1930's.

Steady employment and generally rising wages and salaries
may have played an important part in encouraging the growth
of population, which owing to the restrictions upon immigration was largely a matter of natural increase. The birth rate
rose in the 1940's and went still higher in the 1950's, with the
result that the total population expanded from 140 million in
1945 to over 175 million in 1959. Although special arrangements were made shortly after the end of World War II for the
admission of displaced persons from Europe beyond the normal
immigration quotas, the total so admitted in the period 1946–52
was only 854,000; and in 1950 the native proportion of the

population was 93 per cent—a figure larger than ever before. Further special admission of political exiles in the 1950's is not likely to cause this proportion to decline.

But while the country grew both more populous and more prosperous, the effects of the growth were not uniform in all regions. In some areas industry was stagnant or even in decline, and population grew slowly, if at all; elsewhere, progress was especially rapid. Employment in agricultural occupations continued to decrease, to a total of less than 10 per cent of the entire labor force. New industry developed in the West and to some extent in the South, rather than in the North and East. New England in particular suffered as its manufacturing industry, especially textiles, continued to move to the South in search of cheaper labor and other advantages; and the Pittsburgh region, so long pre-eminent owing to its local supplies of coal, expanded little, while new industrial development concentrated in California and the Gulf states. Internal migration accompanied these changes, and one of the most significant movements was that of Negroes from the rural South to urban areas all over the country, including the West.

Some industries flourished at the expense of others. Petroleum and natural gas production grew while bituminous coal mining declined; trucking and the airlines expanded as railroad transportation contracted. In manufactures, non-durable goods such as textiles, tobacco, and leather all suffered employment decreases; rapid advances, however, took place in chemicals and electronics, and in the manufacture of aircraft and guided missiles. White-collar occupations rose as a proportion of the total, while blue-collar jobs fell off. This was partly due to a rapid rise of employment in finance, insurance, and real estate. But in addition, almost every industry showed a tendency to em-

ploy more professional and technical workers and fewer laborers. Toward the end of the period, disquiet began to be expressed about the possible effects of automation in causing
technological unemployment; but this seemed to be more of a
future prospect than a present reality, except perhaps in the
manufacture of automobiles.

As the general standard of living improved, so the wage-
earner slowly lost his identity as a consumer of cheap, substandard products. With his family, he enjoyed more fully
than ever the opportunities of easier living which could be derived from the ownership of automobiles, television, washing
machines, and refrigerators. He followed the middle-class habit
of moving to the suburbs to obtain improved housing. With
more time for leisure activities, he and his family began to
spend more money on pastimes and on travel. For the white
population, the greatest remaining class differences seemed
to lie in the educational sphere; but here too there was a rapid
expansion of facilities and opportunities. In manners and pattern of everyday life, the nation constantly became more homogeneous. The standard was set by the ever growing middle-
income groups, among whom so many of the wage-earners
had found a place. Yet, as we shall see, the labor unions had a
larger place in American life than ever before.

With the ending of hostilities against Germany in May and
against Japan in August, 1945, numerous wartime contracts
were immediately canceled. Many workers lost their jobs, and
others lost overtime pay and other emergency benefits. As the
servicemen were demobilized, women left their temporary employment and many families suffered a diminution of income.
Since prices continued to rise, it became clear that wage in-

creases were justified to prevent a serious decline in real earnings, and in October President Truman himself spoke in favor of such increases. With more workers looking for jobs, however, and with much uncertainty as to the future, management was unwilling to make concessions. In November Truman held a National Labor-Management Conference, but secured no agreement on proposals to create peacetime machinery for the settlement of industrial disputes. The wartime system of price control, inadequate though it was, remained in existence; and when the War Labor Board went out of existence at the end of the year, it was replaced by a National Wage Stabilization Board, which had the responsibility of deciding on voluntary wage increases for which employers sought compensating price increases. This new board was in operation until early 1947.

It was inevitable after the National Labor-Management Conference that a series of bitter strikes should follow. Indeed they began before the conference dispersed. Truman could do little to prevent them or to hasten their termination, but he appointed fact-finding boards to investigate each major distpute, so as to provide the basis for public pressure on the participants. The United Auto Workers struck against General Motors before the end of November, 1945, and Walter Reuther, who was in charge of the union's General Motors Division, added a novel element to the dispute by demanding the opening of the company's books to show whether or not it could afford the wage increase without alteration of prices. Reuther's demand won some public support for the strikers, which was increased in January when the President's fact-finding board recommended a substantial wage increase—19½ cents an hour. The union was prepared to accept this but the company rejected it as a solution. Just at the same time a steel strike began after last-minute negotiations at the White House had resulted in a very similar situation. Truman had suggested an increase of 18½ cents, which the Steel Workers had accepted on behalf of their members but which the U.S. Steel Corporation had refused. With major strikes also taking place in the electrical and meatpacking industries, the country's manufacturing production was temporarily crippled.

To find a way out of the impasse, in mid-February the administration decided to allow the U.S. Steel Corporation to increase its prices. A settlement could then be made on the basis of Truman's award. This figure became a pattern for settlements in other industries. General Motors yielded the same hourly increase to the Auto Workers, and Chrysler and Ford followed suit. Thus ended the 1945–46 wave of strikes in manufacturing industry, which had been remarkable both for their orderliness and for the deliberate attempts of both sides in each dispute to secure the support of public opinion.

It was not long, however, before two other major disputes developed, one in the coal industry and one on the railroads— both directly involving the federal government. As usual, John L. Lewis' demands outran those of other unions: he sought not only an 18½-cent increase, but also an improved safety code for the mines, and union-controlled health and welfare funds, to be financed by a royalty upon coal production. When these terms were rejected, a strike ensued and the government seized the mines. Lewis now had to negotiate with Julius A. Krug, the Secretary of the Interior, who yielded nearly all that Lewis demanded. Two separate benefit funds were to be set up, one for welfare and retirement payments, which was to be administered jointly by the union and the companies, and the other for medical and hospital purposes, to be run by the union alone. The establishment of these important fringe benefits, although encouraged by the need to find advantages for the workers which would not result in immediate inflationary pressure, also formed an important precedent for the development of collective bargaining patterns in general in the postwar era. The strike on the railroads began in May, when the operating brotherhoods came out after rejecting an arbitration board's award of a 16-cent increase. This was a strike against the government, for as the dispute reached its climax Truman ordered federal seizure. His authority defied by the brotherhoods, the President issued an ultimatum to their leaders to accept his award, and at the same time he demanded emergency legislation from Congress to force them back to work if necessary. The brotherhoods gave way, and the plans for emergency legislation were dropped.

In the summer of 1946 the country was growing weary of its sequence of major strikes; yet it seemed that there would be no end to them, for price increases soon wiped out advantages which the unions had gained. Truman asked Congress to maintain existing price controls for a further year, in the hope of slowing down the inflation; but he was not satisfied with the measure presented to him by Congress in June, and he therefore vetoed it. The result was that price control ended on June 30, and prices at once shot up, in many cases by as much as 25 per cent in two weeks. Congress hastily passed a new measure, no stronger than its predecessor, and this time Truman signed it; but most of the damage had already been done. The cost of living had already risen 6 per cent in a month. The election of a conservative Congress in November forced Truman to conclude that the country preferred freedom from government controls; and later that month he abolished all price restrictions except on rents, sugar, and rice. The result was that by the end of the year the wage increases won in the strikes of the previous fourteen months had been virtually wiped out.

In the fall of 1946 the authority of the government was again tested when John L. Lewis resumed the offensive. Lewis declared void the contract that he had made with the government in May. The government still controlled the mines, and, refusing to make fresh concessions, it secured an injunction against the Mine Workers under the Smith-Connally Act, which had not yet expired. In spite of this, Lewis led the miners out on strike and as a result was found guilty of contempt, his union being fined $3,500,000. Lewis was forced to send the miners back to work, but he appealed the case to the Supreme Court. The Court upheld the conviction, although it reduced the fine to $700,000. In June, 1947, however, the mines were returned to the private owners and Lewis at once obtained a considerably improved contract from them. Meanwhile many of the large industrial unions had been presenting fresh demands based upon the rise in the cost of living and the knowledge of a high level of corporation profits. This time strikes were not usually necessary, for management knew the postwar strength of the unions and preferred to settle on the basis of a 15-cent hourly increase, of which a proportion was earmarked for vacation and other benefits.

Unfortunately for the unions, although all those strikes were not unjustified they inevitably had the effect of alienating public opinion, which tended to blame the strikers and their leaders for the dislocation of industry which resulted from their actions, and also for the price increases that followed. Hostility to the Mine Workers in particular had already reached a high level during the war, and this was continued in the postwar period, when Lewis was again defying the government. The sheer strength of the unions in recent years, as compared with the era before the New Deal, and the persistence of jurisdictional strife, corruption, and intra-union factionalism—particularly Communist factionalism—also contributed to the hostility of the public. In 1946 both Houses of Congress passed the Case bill, which provided for a "cooling-off" period in industrial disputes, outlawed secondary boycotts, permitted unions to be sued for breach of contract, and made welfare funds illegal unless supervised by management as well as labor. This bill was vetoed by the President. But in the November elections of the same year a still more conservative Congress was elected, and fresh legislation seemed inevitable. This took shape as the Taft-Hartley Act, which was passed in June, 1947, over Truman's veto.

The Taft-Hartley Act was a very comprehensive measure. It substantially altered the Wagner Act, by transforming the structure of the N.L.R.B., by specifying the rights of employers in industrial disputes, and by placing many restrictions upon the unions. It also sought to safeguard the rights of individual workers who might not wish to join a union, and to protect the public against undue inconvenience or injury when strikes or lockouts took place. Each of these aspects of the act may be considered in turn.

The reorganization of the N.L.R.B. was for the purpose of insuring the strictly judicial character of its decisions. In the future the board (now to consist of five members instead of three) was to share its functions with a general counsel, who was given sole authority to investigate and prosecute unfair labor practice cases. Although the board retained its responsibility to administer other aspects of the law, such as representation proceedings, it was to act only in a judicial function in cases of unfair labor practice presented to it by the general counsel. This arrangement was more productive of administrative conflict than of judicial impartiality. Much more directly effective were the provisions to specify the rights of employers in industrial disputes with their workers. "Freedom of speech" by employers in addressing their employees on such matters as whether they should join a union was explicitly spelled out.

At the same time, important restrictions and obligations were imposed upon unions. In order to use the facilities of the N.L.R.B., they were required to present to the Secretary of Labor copies of their constitutions and bylaws, lists of the names of their principal officers, and annual financial statements. The members of the unions were also to be furnished with financial reports. In addition, each principal union officer was required every twelve months to file an affidavit that he was not a member of the Communist party and did not believe in violent revolution against the government of the United States. Unions were also forbidden to spend any of their funds on federal elections. The practice of "featherbedding," or introducing "make-work" provisions into union contracts, was declared illegal. Unions were in the future to be liable for the acts of their officials, whether authorized or not, and could henceforth be sued for breach of contract.

In order to safeguard the rights of individual employees, the closed shop was declared illegal, and the union shop (wherein the employer is free to choose his own workers but must fire them if they refuse to join the contracting union) could only be negotiated in fresh contracts if authorized by a majority in a special ballot of the workers. The check-off of union dues by the employer was also forbidden except with the worker's written permission. Workers were to be allowed direct access to their employers in order to air individual grievances; and they were also permitted to ask for elections to withdraw certification of a union as bargaining representative. Craft workers were to be allowed to choose whether to have representation separate from that of other workers in the same plant.

Finally, the public was to be protected by a prohibition of various forms of secondary boycott or strike. The board was to secure injunctions in such cases, and also in stoppages caused by jurisdictional disputes. Strikes and lockouts were to be delayed and, if possible, prevented altogether by provisions for sixty days' notice of demands for alteration or termination of contract—a "cooling-off" period in which the processes of mediation or conciliation might operate. Strikes against the federal government were forbidden altogether. Under the "national emergency strike" procedure the President was given special powers to intervene in stoppages which endanger "the national health or safety," and to order a temporary resumption of work.

Such was the culmination of more than a decade's criticism of the Wagner Act. Although the Taft-Hartley Act was carried with strong support from various anti-labor organizations, including highly interested parties such as the National Association of Manufacturers, it could not have been passed without an enormous change in the climate of public opinion in the period. The attitude of the unions, both before and after it was passed, did not help matters. They condemned it root and branch, and described it as a "slave labor act." Yet many of its provisions, if badly framed, were designed to remove real abuses; and the unions certainly did not wither away as a result of its provisions. For reasons which we have yet to discuss, the tendency has since moved toward imposing even stricter regulations upon the conduct of the unions.

As has already been pointed out, the extent of Communist influence in the unions—almost exclusively in the C.I.O. unions, which were formed in the "red decade" of the 1930's—was a factor in creating public hostility to unionism. The Taft-Hartley Act incorporated clauses designed to reduce or eliminate this influence, which was out of all proportion to actual Communist sympathies among the membership. Just after the end of the war, probably a quarter of the strength of the C.I.O. was under Communist control, and about as much again was on the balance between Communist factions and their opponents. Yet it is doubtful if more than a fraction of 1 per cent of the C.I.O. membership can have consisted of actual members of the party. The success of Communists in the C.I.O. was due entirely to their experience in union agitation at the time when the unions were being formed, to their deliberate efforts as a group to win advantages for themselves, and to the political apathy of the bulk of the membership, in spite of determined efforts by non-Communist elements such as the Socialist Party, now only a shadow of its former self, and the Association of Catholic Trade Unionists (founded in 1937).

The largest of the C.I.O. unions to fall under direct Communist control was the United Electrical Workers, with a membership of about five hundred thousand. Among smaller unions which obeyed the party line were the Mine, Mill, and Smelter Workers (an older union, formerly the Western Federation of Miners, but always noted for its radicalism), the National Maritime Union, the International Longshoremen's and Warehousemen's Union (of the Pacific Coast), the Fur and Leather Workers, and the Farm Equipment Workers. Communist influence was also strong in the United Auto Workers and in the Packinghouse Workers, but not in the Steel Workers, much of whose original leadership had come from John L. Lewis' Mine Workers. Resistance to Communist influence or control quickly grew after the end of World War II as differences arose in the international sphere between the United States and Russia. The election of Walter Reuther as president of the United Auto Workers early in 1946 was an important setback for the Communists; so was the defection of Joseph Curran, president of the National Maritime Union, who after a difficult struggle succeeded in taking his union with him out of Communist control. At the C.I.O. convention late in 1946 President Philip Murray, himself a Catholic, proposed a resolution disavowing Communist control, and this was unanimously carried, as the Communists preferred not to make an issue of it.

In the following year, however, the struggle against the Communists became more acute, partly owing to the intensification of the Cold War and the Communist opposition to American foreign-aid programs, with which the A.F. of L. and the C.I.O. had been invited to associate themselves, and partly as a result of the anti-Communist provisions of the Taft-Hartley Act. In 1947–48 Murray acted to remove individual Communists from influential posts inside the C.I.O. headquarters and exerted disciplinary powers over the local organizations of the C.I.O. or industrial union councils, as they were called. This action was all the more necessary because in 1948 the Communists were backing a third-party candidate in the presidential election—former Vice-President Henry A. Wallace, who stood as a Progressive on a program of conciliation with the Soviet Union. Their hostility to Truman on the issue of foreign affairs was so strong that they refused to support him for re-election, although he pledged himself to do what he could to repeal the Taft-Hartley Act. Truman was indorsed by almost all of organized labor not under Communist control.

The international situation continued to deteriorate, and, owing to the provisions of the Taft-Hartley Act, Communist leadership proved a serious embarrassment to some unions in industrial disputes. Murray decided to eliminate Communism inside the C.I.O. by a frontal attack on its principal stronghold. At the 1949 C.I.O. convention he secured the expulsion of the United Electrical Workers, and also the Farm Equipment Workers with whom the United Auto Workers was engaged in a jurisdictional struggle. He also obtained for the executive board of the C.I.O. authority to investigate and if necessary expel some ten other Communist-dominated unions, most of them small. In most cases, expulsion followed early in 1950; and a new union, the International Union of Electrical Workers, was formed to win the members of the largest expelled organization back to the C.I.O.

This drastic action weakened the C.I.O. numerically for a time but strengthened its unity of purpose. In due course most of the loss of members was made up; by 1955 the new International Union of Electrical Workers had expanded to more than 300,000 members, while the expelled United Electrical Workers was down to some 80,000. A number of the Communist unions lingered on, the strongest of them being the Longshoremen's Union under Harry Bridges, but the total number of members in unions under Communist control had sunk to about 200,000 by 1957.

The C.I.O.'s freedom from Communist control was of considerable importance for the success of American foreign policy in the early years of the Cold War. The government sought the assistance of the labor movement as a whole in the operation of the European Recovery Program; but the World Federation of Trade Unions, which had a Communist secretary-general and an executive with a Communist majority, declared its opposition to the program. As it happened, the C.I.O. was a member of the World Federation, together with the British T.U.C. and other union movements of the non-Communist world; but the A.F. of L. had refused to join when it was founded in 1945, regarding the representation of the government-controlled Russian unions as a fraud. In 1949 the C.I.O. in concert with the T.U.C. and other independent union organizations withdrew from the World Federation and joined with the A.F. of L. in establishing a new world center, the International Confederation of Free Trade Unions. The willingness of the A.F. of L. and the C.I.O. to work together in the same international organization was a new and important development. But the two bodies did not present an entirely united front to the outside world. The A.F. of L. preferred to continue to operate its own international anti-Communist propaganda agency, the Free Trade Union Committee, which it had set up in 1947 under the redoubtable leadership of Jay Lovestone, who had himself been a Communist functionary in the 1920's.

The elimination of Communist influence in the C.I.O. and its collaboration with the A.F. of L. in founding a new world labor organization free of Communist control removed an important obstacle in the way of reconciliation between the two rival centers of the American labor movement. The early 1950's saw decisive action to remove the remaining obstacles to unity.

It has already been pointed out that in the process of competing with the C.I.O. recruiting campaigns, the A.F. of L. unions revived their own organizing militancy and in many cases recruited new members far beyond the bounds of a strict interpretation of craft unionism. As time went on, the C.I.O. unions for their part began more and more to assume the conservative characteristics of well-established labor organizations; the bureaucracy won greater power and there was less influence from the rank and file. In the 1930's many of the C.I.O. leaders were young men in their twenties and thirties; two decades later, there was little to differentiate them from their counterparts in the A.F. of L. In fact, the two national organizations seemed to be divided much more by their inheritance from the past than by any remaining issues of industrial policy.

The expulsion of the Communists from the C.I.O. at once created a more favorable atmosphere for negotiation between the two sides; and the feeling that organized labor was on the defensive against oppressive legislation, as embodied in the Taft-Hartley Act, was an additional factor making for consolidation. Meetings between representatives took place in 1950, but they made little progress at first. The outbreak of the Korean War led to one form of practical collaboration —the establishment of a United Labor Policy Committee, to deal with problems arising from the emergency. This body represented not only the A.F. of L. and the C.I.O. but also the Railway Labor Executives Association, to which the independent railroad brotherhoods belonged, and the International Association of Machinists, which had temporarily disaffiliated from the A.F. of L. But although the committee worked smoothly for some months, it was wrecked by the sudden disaffiliation of the A.F. of L. in August, 1951, on the grounds that it had now fulfilled its task.

Recriminations between the A.F. of L. and the C.I.O. followed this sudden development; and in 1952 the chances of a merger between the two bodies seemed as remote as ever. At the end of the year, however, the situation was transformed by a change of leadership on both sides. Within a month, both President William Green of the A.F. of L. and President Philip Murray of the C.I.O. died, the former at the age of seventy-nine, the latter at sixty-six. Both these men had become somewhat embittered by the conflict between their organizations, and while Green could not conceive of unity except in the form of a return by the C.I.O. unions to "the House of Labor" —that is, to the aegis of the A.F. of L.—Murray for his part was very sensitive about any arrangement which suggested a subordination of his own position to that of Green. Thus both presidents, each of them originally from the Mine Workers, were in their final years acting as obstacles to unity.

The two men who replaced Green and Murray were very different in character. George Meany, who had been secretary-treasurer of the A.F. of L. since 1940, was elected to follow Green as the fourth president of the A.F. of L. Although from a craft union of the building trades—he was a plumber—he was a much stronger personality than Green, and so could be relied upon to exert himself against the exaggerated "autonomy" of the A.F. of L. unions. One of his closest friends was David Dubinsky, the able leader of the International Ladies' Garment Workers, who had helped to found the C.I.O. before returning to the A.F. of L. in 1940. The new president of the C.I.O. was Walter Reuther, who had now been president of the United Auto Workers for six years. Reuther, at forty-five, a dozen years younger than Meany, had been brought up a Socialist and retained a broad conception of the importance of labor solidarity.

Meany at once showed his genuine willingness for unity by declaring, on the day of his election, that the A.F. of L. would reactivate its unity committee and would be prepared to negotiate with the C.I.O. on equal terms. Reuther, who had been elected by only a small majority at the C.I.O. convention, pledged that "vested right in an office" would be no obstacle to his seeking unity. The early months of 1953 therefore saw resumed negotiations, and as a first step a six-man joint committee was appointed to examine the possibility of a no-raiding agreement between the two organizations as a preliminary to unity and also to explore the structural and jurisdictional problems involved in any attempt to make a merger.

The six-man committee started with an analysis of instances of raiding between A.F. of L. and C.I.O. affiliates and discovered that this internecine warfare had brought surprisingly small results for any union in return for a very great expenditure of organizing effort. This fact in itself was an encouragement to both sides to make an armistice, and so the committee was able to draft a no-raiding agreement providing for arbitration of any cases of conflict that arose and also for the formal means of enforcement in the courts. The agreement was made in August, 1953, then approved by the annual conventions of the two bodies, and came into operation in the course of 1954. It ran into some difficulty owing to the failure of some unions, especially in the A.F. of L., to ratify it. The greatest trouble was caused by the Teamsters—a union which was both highly decentralized and very aggressive. The Teamsters had built up their membership by now to 1,200,000, which was as large as any other union in the United States and twice as large as the Teamsters themselves had been at the end of World War II. Nevertheless, the fact that so many unions of both the A.F. of L. and the C.I.O. had ratified the agreement helped to create a much more favorable atmosphere for negotiations on a merger.

As the meetings of the two sides went on, it became clear that Reuther, whose organization was the smaller of the two, was anxious to obtain certain safeguards from the A.F. of L. He wanted guarantees to protect the principle of industrial organization, to insure the observance of the no-raiding agreement by all unions, to eliminate racial discrimination, and to prevent racketeering. Reuther's position was weakened, however, by the insistence of David J. McDonald, the new leader of the Steel Workers and Reuther's principal colleague in the negotiations, that the merger should take place as soon as possible, with or without guarantees. In February, 1955, formal agreement was reached at Miami Beach, just after the conclusion of the A.F. of L. convention there. An Industrial Union Department was to be set up within the merged federation, rather like the existing departments of the A.F. of L. which were designed to deal with jurisdictional and other problems affecting particular industries; and it was decided to establish machinery to secure action against racial discrimination and racketeering. But at the same time, the principle of union autonomy, which had always been basic to the A.F. of L., was explicitly reaffirmed. Lacking effective guarantees, Reuther could only hope that the weight of the C.I.O. unions, combined with that of the more responsible A.F. of L. affiliates, would make itself felt inside the new organization. One favorable omen had been the A.F. of L.'s expulsion of the International Longshoremen's Association in 1953 after the revelations of the New York State Crime Commission.

It remained to draft a constitution and to find a name for the new body. This was done in the course of 1955. Since the A.F. of L. was very anxious to retain its old name, the new body was called "The American Federation of Labor and Congress of Industrial Organizations" (AFL-CIO). The new constitution emphasized the autonomy of affiliates but explicitly stated the equality of status between unions organized on either a craft or an industrial basis. It also specified that unions could be expelled by a two-thirds majority at a convention. Certain situations which would call for disciplinary action were set forth: domination by Communists, Fascists, or other totalitarian groups, or by racketeers or other corrupt influences.

The supreme authority of the AFL-CIO was to be the convention, but this was to meet only once every two years instead of annually as heretofore in both merging organizations. Control between conventions was vested in the executive council, which was given explicit authority to investigate and (with a two-thirds majority) to suspend unions suspected of corrupt or totalitarian influence. This executive council was now to be a large body consisting of the president, the secretary-treasurer, and twenty-seven vice-presidents. A special general board was constituted, consisting of one representative —usually the president—of each affiliated national union. This body was designed to serve as a convenient sounding-board of the affiliates in the interval between conventions. The size of the executive council necessitated the creation of a small executive committee of six vice-presidents, in addition to the president and the secretary-treasurer. By the terms of the merger, George Meany and William F. Schnitzler, president and secretary-treasurer of the A.F. of L., were to retain their posts in the new body. The whole complicated structure was designed to insure that adequate representation was given to all elements constituting the AFL-CIO.

The constitution naturally arranged for the merger of the state and city federations of the two organizations, although very wisely a period of two years was allowed for this to be completed. (In a great many cases the process took considerably longer.) Local unions directly subordinate to the AFL-CIO were also provided for. A department of organization was set up, and also a series of committees on various subjects including civil rights, political education—a euphemism for political action—and ethical practices. Dues to the AFL-CIO were to be at the former A.F. of L. level of 4 cents a month for each member, which was much lower than the former C.I.O. level of 10 cents. But the affiliates of the industrial union department—mostly former C.I.O. unions— were to pay an additional 2 cents to the department. It was hoped that the economies that would eventually result from the merger would justify the drop in the total income of the merged organizations. Obviously, much depended not only upon the forms of the constitution but also upon the men who would put them into practice.

With the accomplishment of the merger, the country had a united movement which was more fully representative of

American labor than any which had preceded it. The very fact of unity was an indication that the old ethnic divisions had lost their significance. With the numerical decline of first-generation immigrants as a proportion of the population, the old differences based upon European origin were becoming a thing of the past. It is true, however, that racial discrimination remained to qualify the growing social homogeneity of the nation; and this was reflected in the labor movement by the maintenance of the color bar in practice in many locals, especially in the South. This was much more common in former A.F. of L. unions than in those which had belonged to the C.I.O. Many of the latter had a particularly good record in fighting racial discrimination. The old independent railroad brotherhoods also retained their constitutional bans on the admission of Negroes, and the two brotherhoods of Locomotive Firemen and of Trainmen, which joined the AFL-CIO in 1956–57, were not compelled to remove their bans as a condition of joining. The committee on civil rights, although prodded to take action on various cases by the National Association for the Advancement of Colored People, for the first few years after the merger decided to move very cautiously, no doubt feeling that little progress could be made until the other internal stresses and strains of the new body had eased a little. Sooner or later, however, the pressure of the two million Negroes already inside the AFL-CIO was sure to make itself felt.

Unquestionably the most serious problem facing the AFL-CIO in its early years was that of corruption. As we have seen, in 1953 the A.F. of L. had expelled the International Longshoremen's Association when a state commission had revealed its links with the underworld. The A.F. of L. executive had then proceeded to set up a rival organization to try to win away the membership of the corrupt union, but in spite of lavish expenditure of organizing funds it had failed to obtain certification in N.L.R.B. elections at the New York docks. Nevertheless, the act of expulsion provided a valuable precedent for the AFL-CIO ethical practices committee, which proceeded to draw up a series of codes of behavior, condemning undemocratic procedures by union officers, misuse of funds, collusive contracts, and so on. The committee's first disciplinary actions were to press the Teamsters not to enter into financial relations with the Longshoremen's Association, and to invite the Allied Industrial Workers (formerly the United Auto Workers, A.F. of L.), the Distillery Workers, the Laundry Workers and the Bakery and Confectionery Workers to remove the corrupt elements which they contained.

The committee was of course limited in the amount of evidence of corruption that it could obtain, for it could not subpoena witnesses. Early in 1957, however, the issue was taken up by the Senate of the United States, which established a "Select Committee on Improper Activities in the Labor or Management Field" under the chairmanship of Senator John L. McClellan of Arkansas. The Senate committee, with the assistance of an able chief counsel, Robert F. Kennedy, soon uncovered a vast network of corruption in the Teamsters Union at all levels up to and including the president, Dave Beck, who was also a vice-president of the AFL-CIO.

A few months later the AFL-CIO ethical practices committee formally indicted Beck and the Teamsters, and undertook its own investigation of another union in which the McClellan Committee had found corruption, the United Textile Workers, as well as those unions which it had already warned to clean up. It also urged Congress to pass legislation to insure honesty of management in welfare and pension funds, which had rapidly grown in size and number in the previous decade. Beck, who was indicted by a federal grand jury for income-tax evasion and illegal phone-tapping, decided to retire from the presidency of the Teamsters, but when the Teamsters' convention met in the fall of 1957 it elected as his successor a man who had aroused almost equal distaste at the McClellan Committee's hearings—namely, James R. Hoffa of Detroit. On the recommendation of the executive council, therefore, the Teamsters were expelled by the AFL-CIO convention in December, together with the Bakery and Confectionery Workers and the Laundry Workers. The Allied Industrial Workers were restored to full standing and it was reported that the United Textile Workers were complying with demands for reform. The Distillery Workers remained on probation.

Thus the AFL-CIO acted promptly to dissociate itself as an organization from the racket-ridden elements disclosed by its own inquiries and by the McClellan Committee. This did not, however, prevent the public from identifying the rackets with the whole labor movement, even though some of the McClellan Committee evidence had implicated nationally known corporation managements as well as labor leaders. It was true of course that whereas the management representatives were simply "making the fast buck," presumably for their stockholders, the labor leaders concerned were lining their own pockets at the expense of the union membership.

In the legislative sphere, therefore, the unions were on the defensive, and any prospect of a return to the favorable political climate of the Wagner Act receded constantly into the background throughout the 1950's. The A.F. of L. and the C.I.O. would have done better in the late 1940's if they had concentrated on the amendment, rather than on the total repeal, of the Taft-Hartley Act; for even Senator Taft, its sponsor, was willing to make important concessions on such matters as legalizing the "union hiring hall," which was a convenience to both unions and management where casual labor was employed, and also permitting certain forms of the secondary boycott, which in some industries were an essential element of the unions bargaining strength. When President Eisenhower, on taking office in 1953, appointed a unionist, Martin P. Durkin, to the office of Secretary of Labor, it seemed for a time as if amendments on these lines would be sponsored by the administration. But the death of Senator Taft caused the abandonment of plans for new legislation, and Durkin resigned shortly afterward. The only amendment of the Act to take place was the abandonment in 1951 of the requirement of a ballot conducted by the N.L.R.B. before a union-shop contract could be negotiated.

During most of the 1950's, with a Republican and conservative Democratic coalition ruling in Congress, labor lobbyists were hard put to it to prevent the enactment of even stricter legislation. There was also a danger that the "right to work" principle, which had been enacted in many of the less industrialized states in 1947, would spread to the states which contained the main centers of union strength. These laws made illegal not only the closed shop but also the union shop and other forms of union security. A law of this type was enacted in Indiana in 1957, and similar legislation would have been passed in other states, including California, had not the unions made great exertions at the 1958 elections.

In the summer of 1959, after more than two years of investigations by the McClellan Committee, public opinion demanded legislative action to curb union corruption. After a radio address by President Eisenhower, the two Houses of Congress finally agreed on a measure which was a compromise between a "tough" bill proposed by Representatives Landrum and Griffin and the more liberal reforming sentiments of Senator Kennedy and a number of his colleagues. The compromise measure was much more restrictive, however, than anything that the AFL-CIO itself was prepared to support. Its main provisions laid down precise regulations for the procedure of union elections and for the supervision of all financial matters. It also outlawed extortion picketing and almost all forms of secondary boycott. At the same time, however, liberal amendments provided safeguards for union security provisions in the construction industry and for the protection of unions in the construction and the garment industries against non-union subcontracting. In addition, the states were authorized to exercise jurisdiction over categories of cases not dealt with by the N.L.R.B., thus eliminating a "no man's land" where previously no legislation had operated.

The passing of this measure clearly marked the beginning of a new era for the unions. On the whole, the act seemed likely to achieve its main purpose of preventing the major forms of corruption without seriously endangering the freedom of the unions to organize and bargain. Known officially as the Labor-Management Reporting and Disclosure Act, it really deserves the title of "Hoffa's Act," for the truculence

George Meany (*center*) and Walter Reuther link hands at the merger convention of the AFL-CIO, 1957. (Courtesy, AFL-CIO News.)

James R. Hoffa, president of the International Brotherhood of Teamsters, gives evidence before the McClellan Committee, 1958. (United
Press International Photo.)

of the Teamsters' president before the McClellan Committee was probably the decisive element in securing its passage.

At the end of the 1950's the American labor movement could claim a membership of almost 18 million, which was a little more than a quarter of the total civilian labor force of 70 million, or over a third of the 50 million eligible to join. For several years, union strength remained constant as a proportion of the population. There seemed to be special difficulties in making recruits beyond the citadels provided by the larger urban areas of the North and West, or outside the blue-collar occupations in these areas. The South continued to resist unionism, its opponents often accusing the organizers —rather ironically, in some cases—of being the agents of racial integration. In small towns and in the countryside generally, the climate of opinion was hostile, and very few agricultural laborers were organized. Furthermore—and this was the most serious feature of all, in view of the occupational trends of the 1950's—comparatively few white-collar workers belonged to unions. The AFL-CIO seemed to face the prospect of having to struggle hard to maintain its membership in what was a steadily declining proportion of the total population, the blue-collar workers of the mass-production industries of the North, together with the building and some sections of the transportation workers of the same areas.

The public image of the labor movement was rather different from this. The McClellan Committee hearings had built up the bogey of a brutally strong movement, bullying small employers who were obliged to yield it blackmail. While this might be true of the Teamsters—which alone among the large unions had expanded its membership steadily throughout the period—it was very rarely true of unions in other industries, which were normally either small themselves or, if large like the Auto Workers and the Steel Workers, had even larger corporations to deal with. Indeed, the prolonged steel strike in the later months of 1959 showed convincingly that the national interest could suffer as much from the intransigence of employers as from the aggressiveness of union leaders.

Even in the case of the larger unions, it must be borne in mind that the great bulk of union activity took place at the local level. There the organization frequently depended as it always had on the voluntary, unpaid efforts of men and women who were themselves manual workers—the "Jimmie Higginses" of whom Upton Sinclair once wrote. For them, unionism remained a matter of personal devotion largely without reward; and for many of the workers whom they served, theirs was, as it always had been, the "face" of the union. It would usually be the shop committeeman, not the full-time union official, who would secure the individual, unremarked act of reparation or compassion—the remedy of a grievance, or the overlooking of an error—by which the average worker judges the value of his union membership.

It would be unfair, moreover, not to acknowledge the success that many unions had had in securing the preservation of democratic practices and honest management in the face of strong pressures. Thus the International Typographical Union (whose leaders voted against the expulsion of the Teamsters in order to preserve the principle of union autonomy) possessed a two-party system in union elections, in which the rights of the "opposition" were effectively guaranteed. The International Ladies' Garment Workers and the Clothing Workers had both had to struggle hard against the infiltration of racketeers into their locals, but both unions established unique records as pioneers in securing the welfare of their members. The Clothing Workers owned the only successful union banks, and the Ladies' Garment Workers were noted for their educational and health programs. Countless other unions could claim a record of steady and honest service, which never hit the headlines of the national press. Such enormous contrasts inside one movement defy generalization, and should serve to remind us that the structure of labor unionism, now as in the past, reflects the variety of American life itself.

IX

The Permanent Minority

In the first chapter of this book an attempt was made to list the characteristics of labor in the colonial period, and it was suggested that the same features, or some of them, might be found persisting throughout American history up to the present day. Let us look back at our story and endeavor to assess this element of continuity.

First of all, there was the variety of circumstance attending the American worker, which arose from the wide range of geographical conditions in the already large area of the colonies and from the different ethnic and social backgrounds from which the earlier settlers and their servants came. This variety, as we saw, began to diminish somewhat in the early national period as communications improved, as indentured servitude ended, and as the different elements of the population began to intermingle and become "Americanized." Yet for the Negroes who remained as slaves it did not disappear, and as the trickle of immigration in the early nineteenth century grew into a vast and variegated torrent, it became significant again for the white population as a whole. In the later years of the nineteenth century, changes in the source of immigration added new and different elements to the ethnic mixture and brought fresh problems of adjustment and assimilation. The decision to restrict immigration was made, significantly enough, at a time of national crisis caused by World War I and its aftermath. Whatever its merits, this was indeed the only way of providing the circumstances in which a relatively homogeneous labor force could develop in the United States.

Inevitably, the form of labor organization reflected these ethnic, racial, and geographical differences. Sidney and Beatrice Webb, writing of the British labor movement, classified the practices of unionism as either exclusive or inclusive in character. Most characteristic of the former was the attempt to restrict entry into a craft by high initiation fees, strict apprenticeship regulation, and so on, while the latter usually took the form of establishing, either by industrial or by political action, a "Common Rule" of minimum wages or conditions to which all employers were obliged to adhere. Because of the barriers of language and custom which separated American workers from one another and because of the sheer size of the country and the complexity of its political institutions, it was much easier for the unions to employ exclusive rather than inclusive practices. According to Selig Perlman, whose views have long dominated the generally accepted interpretation of American labor history, this tendency toward exclusive practices was a sign of the "maturity" of the American "trade union mentality." It is doubtful, however, whether the excluded workers saw it in the same light.

For the fact was that the practices of exclusion could best

be carried out not by apprenticeship regulations, which in the face of rapid technical change were always difficult to enforce, but rather by direct discrimination against immigrants or Negroes, whether or not they had the necessary qualifications for union membership. The union label, perhaps the most important American contribution to the technique of unionism, originated in an attempt to restrict the competition of Chinese labor in California. The first label said, "The cigars contained in this box are made by WHITE MEN." In various other crafts, especially the building trades, discrimination operated against Jewish craftsmen, who were obliged to limit themselves to the less desirable work on alterations instead of on new construction, thus bringing into existence various local unions of "alteration carpenters" and so on. Some unions barred the admission of Negroes by constitutional provision; others effected it by local custom. Some unions, to keep out immigrants, made the possession of citizenship a definite prerequisite of membership; others merely levied exceptionally high initiation fees on foreigners.

John R. Commons, the distinguished labor historian, declared on one occasion that the unions performed a valuable function in "Americanizing" the immigrant, accustoming him to the processes of democratic control, and in some cases inducing him to learn the English language. Yet elsewhere in his work Commons suggested that the emphasis placed on the closed shop by American unions, so much stronger than in Britain and elsewhere, was a result of their anxiety to put some limitation on a labor supply that was constantly being inflated by immigration. Evidently, therefore, if the unions performed an "Americanizing" function it was a service done reluctantly and, in some trades, very rarely if at all. On the contrary, in occupations with a substantial proportion of immigrant workers there was likely to be a process of a reverse kind—namely, the "Balkanization" of the unions concerned as a result of their recruitment of immigrants unable to speak English or to understand American ways.

On the one hand, it was necessary for unions in this situation to organize special foreign-language locals; and if the particular ethnic element concerned was substantial enough, these locals of various trades might unite in the larger cities into federations, such as the United German Trades, the United Hebrew Trades, or the Italian Chamber of Labor. On the other hand, where foreign-speaking immigrants, unused to the American environment, were placed in subordination to the officers of established unions, they were readily open to exploitation, sometimes merely by losing their democratic rights of election inside the union, and sometimes also by being forced to accept unnecessarily unfavorable contracts.

As the American population has become more homogeneous in recent years, so the disruptive effects of ethnic rivalry upon the formal unity of the movement have ceased to have so much importance. This change helped to make possible the reunion of the two major national federations of labor into one single organization, the AFL-CIO. Yet the heritage of the past remains, in the form of unions with conflicting jurisdictions, suspicious of each other and unable to combine owing to remaining prejudices and to the vested interest of the officials concerned. Worst of all, of course, is the racial discrimination which continues to prevent Negroes from joining certain unions or forces them into separate Jim Crow locals. So far, the AFL-CIO civil rights committee has had little success in changing existing practices of this type.

American Labor

Of the economic origins of this anti-Negro prejudice we need have no doubt. Throughout American history, it has been most acute among national groups directly competing for the same jobs. At the time of the Civil War, for instance, it was the Irish, in those days mostly unskilled laborers, who were the readiest to set upon the Negroes; a half-century later, it was the Poles. The willingness of Negroes to serve as strikebreakers often exacerbated the hostility; and this willingness can in turn be explained by the Negroes' desperate need for employment and by the many rebuffs that they had suffered at the hands of the unions which had discriminated against them. In the 1920's the packinghouse employers of Chicago not only used Negroes as strikebreakers but also organized them subsequently into a special company union called rather ironically the American Unity Labor League. It was only in the 1930's, with the new beginning of unionism in the mass-production industries, that all races began to be organized into the same industrial unions. So far as the craft unions founded earlier are concerned, however, the struggle for equal rights is by no means won. The marginal status of Negro workers even in recent years is clearly indicated by the fact that in the later 1950's their unemployment rate was twice that for the white worker.

Another characteristic of American labor during the colonial period was the high wage rate of the free craftsman or laborer, compared with that of his counterpart in Europe. At first, as we saw, the difference was in part a premium arising from the expense of the Atlantic journey which brought the worker to America from the land of his birth. But so long as American resources in land and industry remained easier to exploit than those elsewhere, this differential advantage was bound to remain. It was Thomas Carlyle who attributed the happy state of the American laborer to the fact that there was "a vost deal of land for a verra few people"; since his day, however, historians have come to doubt how far this factor remained of importance in the nineteenth century. But even if the land was not quite as freely available as has generally been supposed, the rapid expansion of industrial resources, at a pace far exceeding that of the other countries of the world, kept American wages high and stimulated further immigration.

It is difficult to be sure exactly how much higher, on the average, American wages were at particular times than those prevailing in Europe; statistics are incomplete and comparison is consequently difficult, especially as allowance must be made for differing costs of living. Probably there were always some immigrants who found life more difficult in America than at home, but by and large the newcomers reckoned that the wages they received more than compensated for the extra cost of living they encountered. In the twentieth century, we are on firmer ground in making numerical comparisons. We know, for instance, that in 1940 the wages per hour of the average unskilled laborer in the United States and Canada were about 60 per cent above those of similar workers in Great Britain, Switzerland, and Scandinavia, and that the differential was even larger in all other countries except Australia. The effect of World War II was, of course, to increase the gap still further in favor of the United States.

It cannot be maintained that unionism has contributed significantly to the continual progression of wage increases that have taken place in the course of American history. The proportion of organized workers was so small until a generation ago that they could hardly dictate to the economy as a whole. Rather, the determining factors were those already outlined —the comparative shortage of manpower in relation to resources and the advances in productivity which enabled employers to make major concessions in order to maintain an effective labor force. It may well be that the continuing shortage of labor and its consequent high cost played an important part in causing managements to experiment with labor-saving devices, which in turn had a favorable influence upon productivity and enabled the wage-level to rise still further.

Since the New Deal period, which saw the great expansion of unionism, the wage-structure has undergone much change. In comparison with the skilled, the unskilled workers have improved their position considerably. To a large extent, however, this change is the result of the decline in immigration and the enactment of federal minimum wage legislation, although it is reasonable to assume that the influence of the new industrial unions, which has tended in the same direction, has not been entirely without effect. There still remains, in any case, a wide gulf between the "aristocrats" of the labor world, such as the steel mill rollers who may earn $12,000 a year, and at the other extreme the "untouchable" class of migratory workers, little affected by social legislation, who may often fail to gross $2,000 a year per family for the work of two adults and one or more children.

Yet the fact that the average standard of living is higher in the United States than elsewhere tends of itself to make differences of income and wealth less obvious. What is important is the elimination of glaring contrasts in consumption patterns which inevitably exist in a poor country, even if its system of distribution is comparatively equalitarian. As Gunnar Myrdal has pointed out, "It is indeed a regular occurrence endowed almost with the dignity of an economic law that the poorer the country, the greater the difference between poor and rich."

Moreover, the continuously rising incomes of almost all major occupational groups in the United States cannot be doubted, and this fact inevitably prevents the emergence of much industrial or political militancy on the part of the workers. Increasingly in recent years union leaders have found it convenient to take more and more of the gains that they make in collective bargaining in the form of the reduction of hours and in fringe benefits such as pensions, supplemental unemployment benefits, paid vacations, and health and welfare plans. The development of fringe benefits started in wartime, when there was an obligation to avoid the inflationary pressure that would have been caused by direct wage increases; but the postwar period has seen a vast expansion in the same direction. If to some extent it argues an inadequacy of federal and state provision for social security, it also suggests that direct increases in wage levels have ceased to hold the overriding importance that was once attached to them.

From the earliest beginnings of American society we noted the importance of the agricultural background in shaping the life of the worker. It is true that in the twentieth century this had ceased to be of great importance, but it remained true throughout the nineteenth century that a considerable majority of the population lived in rural surroundings. At the time of the 1900 census the proportion was still over 60 per cent, and it was not until 1920 that it could be said that more than half the population lived in cities or towns of twenty-five hundred inhabitants or more.

The significance of this rural background will be appreciated if the unique character of American agricultural life is borne in mind. The typical American farmer was an independent man, often owning his own farm and working it himself and with his family. He relied little on outside assistance, so that except in the South and to some extent in the Far West there was never any substantial American class of landless laborers, as in Britain, nor any miserable peasantry bowed down by feudal dues, as in eighteenth-century France, or Russia through the ages. In colonial times, and perhaps much later as well, the urban worker was more likely than not a person who had been raised in the countryside and who often had the aspiration to return to it by investing his savings in the establishment or purchase of a homestead. The first factory workers, indeed, were in many cases girls from farming families who spent only a limited part of their lives in the mills and whose general standard of education and health was far above that of the large urban proletariat which was then characteristic of British industry. Far into the nineteenth century it remained possible for the American worker to set his sights at an escape into rural life, possibly in the immediately surrounding countryside, but more likely in the West, where land was still cheap and agriculture was a developing occupation. Whether or not we hold to the theory that the West was a "safety valve" for urban labor, the effect of such aspirations upon the solidarity of the American working class must have been considerable.

The existence of a large class of farmers who were neither

rich nor poor tended to provide an important stabilizing force in American society, and in the late eighteenth century there were many who feared that the development of industry would destroy this stabilizing force. Had they lived until the seventies and eighties of the nineteenth century, no doubt they would have felt that the riots and strikes of those years justified their fears. Looking at American social development as a whole, however, we can see that industrial violence though recurrent for half a century was not to become normative, that the inheritance from earlier generations was not lost or abandoned.

In the political sphere, the federal Constitution and the conservatism of electoral reapportionment perpetuated the influence of the countryside as against the cities. This meant that there remained a strong pressure group representing the farmers and other rural interests, which was poised between capital and labor, throwing its weight either to one side or the other, but never consistently to either. When the farmers were themselves suffering from depression and deeply concerned about the monopoly power of the railroads and other large corporations, the conditions existed for an alliance between them and the forces of urban labor. This took shape both locally and nationally at the time of the Greenback agitation, during the Populist period, and again, to a certain extent, in the Progressive and New Deal epochs.

Mention of Progressivism and of the New Deal reminds us, however, that as the agrarian element weakened in the twentieth century, the components of the alliances which labor could join became more and more urban in character. The weakening of rural political influence was made up for by the growth of professional and middle-class interests distinct from those of large-scale business. One characteristic remained throughout this change: the minority position of labor, which was dependent upon the temporary and evanescent support of other political groups in order to secure legislation for its own benefit.

At various times in the past it has seemed as if the United States might be transformed into a country with an actual predominance of urbanized manual workers, like Britain; and consequently the advent of a political organization like the British Labour party was confidently anticipated. A variety of factors may be adduced for the failure of the American labor unions to form a labor party, but the most important of all has been the fact that at no time have the urban blue-collar workers actually constituted a majority of the population. The old agrarian predominance in American society has passed, to be replaced by an urban middle-class predominance. In 1956, for the first time, the number of white-collar workers in industry exceeded that of blue-collar workers, without taking the farmers into account. Labor leaders thus have to accept the fact that their traditional constituency, so far from increasing, is actually in decline as a proportion of the total population.

Being always a minority, therefore, the American labor movement suffers many political vicissitudes. In times of economic depression it can usually rely not only upon the greater loyalty of its own members to labor's political interests but also upon a sudden rise of reforming enthusiasm in other quarters. Hence came the great periods of social change under Woodrow Wilson and Franklin D. Roosevelt, including the enactment of legislation favoring the expansion of the unions. At other times, however, and particularly when the country is especially prosperous, the unions may find themselves deprived of the accessions to membership that they might normally expect, not only because their prospective members are inclined to feel more independent, but also because the progressive or liberal alliance upon which organized labor has relied has fallen away, leaving it exposed to a hostile legislative and judicial climate, as in the 1920's or in the later 1940's and 1950's. Moreover, whatever the political situation of the time, it has been noteworthy that organized labor has never been able to secure public approval to the extent of being able to place its own leaders in major federal offices. The post of Secretary of Labor, it is true, may occasionally go to a unionist, and a few may serve in the House of Representatives; but the established concept of the unions' role in politics is that it should be confined to the lobbies, that it must act as a pressure group and not attempt to take over the functions of a party. Exactly the same is true of their role in individual states, even in a strongly industrialized state such as New York or Michigan.

The final permanent characteristic of American labor, which really emerges from those which we have already discussed, is its lack of class consciousness. Obviously, this is in part a product of ethnic and racial rivalries, and of the divisive effect of different social conditions in different parts of the country. It also owes a great deal to the factor of high wages, which has enabled American workers to exhibit many of the same consumption and behavior patterns as those of other social groups. And we may be sure that the ease with which workers could become farmers had a great effect in earlier years in preventing them from becoming conscious of grievances as a class.

American Labor

It may reasonably be argued that in the twentieth century a good deal of the old social mobility of the American people has been lost. This is not only because of the almost complete loss of agricultural opportunities. The absence of a continued flow of new immigrants, adding a "push" from below to the "pull" of other social factors from above, must be considered of major importance. It is true of course that the public school system, as a force making for social coherence, remains; but more and more significance now attaches to education at a higher level, and here the system is less uniform and less complete. Recent studies have shown that in the past generation social mobility has hardly been greater in the United States than in certain countries of western Europe, particularly those with the highest average standard of living, such as Britain and Scandinavia.

Traditionally, however, it was of great importance for the United States that class consciousness was weak and that political theories based upon the concept of class never obtained very much hold. The American worker was voting for the Whigs or the Democrats at a time when European workers were almost uniformly without the franchise, and his children were being educated when most children in other countries grew up as illiterates. He had no great inclination therefore to make as much of class distinction as was made of it elsewhere.

It is true of course that some later groups of immigrants, particularly the Germans and East European Jews, brought with them a belief in Marxian Socialism, which they had developed under the rule of the Hohenzollerns, the Hapsburgs, and the Romanovs. For a time, these immigrants and also their children, the second generation in America, gave considerable support to the Socialist movement, and provided the bulk of the membership for both De Leon's Socialist Labor Party and for the more moderate Socialist Party of America under Debs, Hillquit, and others. In 1917, the Socialist Party reported a total of 80,126 members, of whom no less than 32,894 were actually organized in special foreign-language federations. Indeed, their high proportion of foreign members proved to be the undoing of the Socialist parties, for they could so easily be attacked during World War I for pursuing a policy to suit the interests of the countries of their origin rather than those of the United States. The bitterness caused by these attacks and the dissensions occasioned by the Bolshevik Revolution in Russia led to the disintegration of Socialism as a force of even moderate importance in American politics.

There have been times, indeed, when something closely akin to class conflict in the Marxian sense seemed to predominate in the industrial life of the country. The rapid growth of large, impersonal industrial corporations in the 1870's and 1880's, which proceeded to replace an established labor force by a systematic recruitment of unskilled immigrants, certainly led to much bitterness and, in some cases, owing to the weakness of law enforcement, to bloodshed. The use of private police, of industrial espionage, and of strong-arm methods to destroy unionism naturally provoked the emergence of equally violent elements inside the labor movement, of whom the "Molly Maguires" may have been early instances, though they were more obviously exemplified by the Western Federation of Miners and the I.W.W.

Even as late as 1922 a complete failure of law enforcement in Illinois could lead to the deaths of twenty-three men, mostly strikebreakers, in the "Herrin massacre." But we must not make the mistake of assuming that this type of conflict was ever characteristic of American industrial relations as a whole. Rather it tended to be, as Selig Perlman has pointed out, more a product of frontier conditions in the West than the result of a confrontation of established social classes such as might occur in a stratified society. The present century has seen the gradual elimination of most of these harsh features of the past, partly through the great growth of federal legislation on social and industrial questions and partly as a result of the emergence of a professional managerial class, which has learned either to accept the processes of collective bargaining or to devise subtler methods of competing with the unions. Visiting teams of unionists from Europe, who came to study American industry under the auspices of the Marshall Plan, commented upon the informality of relationships between management and workers, which was hardly what they had come to expect from their reading of the novels of Jack London, Upton Sinclair, and the like.

In some respects, it must be acknowledged, the weakness of class consciousness in America and the ease with which social barriers may be crossed is a cause of embarrassment to the labor movement. Particularly in industries which have a large number of small employers, such as the building trades, the garment industry, and trucking, it has exposed union officials to greater temptations of corruption than would come their way in a more class-conscious society. In other industrial countries the labor leader senses a considerable gap of manners and behavior between himself and the businessmen with whom he deals, and both he and they may thereby be inhibited from making collusive contracts or other corrupt arrangements at the expense of the workers. For the labor leader, certainly, the crime would be both more heinous and easier to detect; few European union officials, however prominent, could expect to rival the way of life of even the moderately prosperous businessman, and so any additional affluence resulting from corruption would at once be evident. In the United States, on the other hand, where the salaries of international presidents and secretary-treasurers and even of the officers of some local unions run far into five figures, all check upon conspicuous consumption by labor leaders has long since disappeared.

At the same time, American labor leaders have had a deeper appreciation of the problems of management than their counterparts in other countries; and this has sometimes helped them to develop exceptional influence, greatly to the benefit of their bargaining position. In no other country have the unions penetrated so deeply into the responsibilities normally restricted to management as they have in several American industries—particularly those industries, once again, which contain a large number of small and highly competitive firms. The unions freely employ staff experts of all sorts—economists, public relations men, and lawyers—and are not afraid to give them salaries commensurate with their worth. With the advice of these experts they are often in a position to assume a paternalistic attitude to the small employer who does not have comparable resources. The Amalgamated Clothing Workers, indeed, has provided its employers with technical assistance in improving shop efficiency and has won control over a wide area of industrial and pricing policy as well as over personnel matters. If this degree of influence is exceptional, it is nevertheless true that by reason of their approximation to the status, manners, and affluence of business executives, union leaders have been able to make more effective use of their industrial strength in America than in other more narrowly class-conscious societies.

What, then of the future? It may appear to the general public that the American labor movement is henceforth going to play an ever greater part in the nation's affairs. When the AFL-CIO merger took place, much was written on the threat of a "labor monopoly" to the economic and political life of the country; and the lavishness of the new union headquarters, many of them located in Washington within easy reach of the nation's legislators, may seem to confirm this impression.

Yet, as we have seen, the ties that bind the union member to his union are no stronger now than they have been in the past, rather less so in all likelihood; and the chances of recruiting many more members in proportion to the total labor force do not seem favorable. As the workers move out to the suburbs and assume more and more of the characteristics of the middle class, the possibility that they will operate as an effective political force diminishes. Great gains may yet be made for the unions in the South, but probably not without compensating proportionate losses in the North as the industrial labor force there declines. Barring the return of economic distress on the scale experienced in the 1930's, it is difficult to believe that organized labor will escape from the minority position that it has always in practice been limited to, or that manual workers as a whole will become any more distinct than now from the larger whole of American society.

Within the limits set by these considerations, however, the leaders of organized labor have very important tasks to perform. They have to fight as they have done in the past for the economic and social interests of their members, whose position certainly might otherwise be undermined. And they know well enough now that the success of this struggle must depend upon their retaining the respect of public opinion. The very fact that the labor movement is at the moment in some sense a scapegoat for what is really a national problem—the prevalence of corruption and racketeering in many parts of the economy—should make them redouble their efforts to set a high standard of ethical behavior. The initiative which has been displayed by the leaders of the AFL-CIO since the merger suggests that the prospects for the accomplishment of this aim are good.

Important Dates

1621–23	Wage scales established in Virginia
1630–33	Maximum wages set in Massachusetts
1648	Boston Coopers and Shoemakers Gilds founded
1676	Bacon's Rebellion, Virginia, by indentured servants
1707	British Parliament systematizes criminal servitude
1778	Successful strike of journeymen printers, New York City
1792	Philadelphia shoemakers form local union
1794	New York City typographers form local union
1806	Philadelphia shoemakers found guilty of criminal conspiracy for forming a union and striking
1827	Mechanics Union of Trade Associations formed at Philadelphia—the first recorded city central body
1828	Workingmen's party formed at Philadelphia
1829	Workingmen's party formed in New York City
1831	Slave insurrection in Virginia led by Nat Turner
1833	American Anti-Slavery Society formed
1834	National Trades Union formed in New York—the first attempt at a national federation of trades
	Locofoco party formed in New York
1836	New York Journeymen Tailors' Case: unionism again found to be an illegal conspiracy
1840	Ten-hour day established for federal employees by executive order of President Van Buren

Important Dates

1842	*Commonwealth* v. *Hunt:* Massachusetts Supreme Court holds labor unions not illegal conspiracies
1852	Typographical Union founded—the earliest national union to remain in permanent existence
1859	Iron Molders Union founded, largely by William Sylvis
1860	Successful strike of some twenty thousand New England shoemakers
1863	Slavery emancipation
	Brotherhood of Locomotive Engineers founded
1866	National Labor Union formed
1867	Knights of St. Crispin (shoemakers) formed
1868	Congress enacts eight-hour day for federal employees
1869	Knights of Labor founded at Philadelphia
1875	Conviction of "Mollie Maguires" for coalfield murders; ten hanged
1876	Workingmen's Party, later Socialist Labor Party, founded
1877	Railroad strikes in Philadelphia and elsewhere cause many deaths, use of federal troops
1878	Greenback Labor Party wins over a million votes in congressional elections
1879	Terence V. Powderly elected Grand Master Workman of Knights of Labor
1881	Federation of Organized Trades and Labor Unions founded
1882	First Labor Day celebration in New York City, on initiative of P. J. McGuire
1884	Federal Bureau of Labor established
1885	Foran Act forbids immigration of laborers on contract
1886	Eight-hour movement: Haymarket bomb outrage (one policeman killed, others wounded)
	American Federation of Labor founded as successor to Federation of Organized Trades: Samuel Gompers elected president
1887	Seven Anarchists sentenced to death (five actually die) for Haymarket outrage
1888	International Association of Machinists founded
1890	United Mine Workers founded
1892	Strike at Carnegie steel mills, Homestead, Pa.; twelve Pinkertons and strikers killed

| 1894 | Pullman strike by Debs's American Railway Union; strike broken with injunctions, use of federal troops; Debs jailed for contempt |

National Association of Manufacturers founded

1898 Erdman Act passed, providing for mediation and voluntary arbitration on the railroads

Holden v. *Hardy:* Supreme Court upholds Utah state law, limiting hours for miners

U.S. Industrial Commission set up (final report 1901)

1900 International Ladies' Garment Workers' Union founded

1901 Amalgamated Association of Iron, Steel, and Tin Workers defeated in five-month strike against U.S. Steel Corp.

Foundation of Socialist Party of America

1902 Anthracite coal strike: presidential commission appointed to arbitrate

1905 Industrial Workers of the World (I.W.W.) founded

1908 Danbury Hatters Case: Supreme Court holds a boycott to be in restraint of trade under the Sherman Antitrust Act (1890)

Muller v. *Oregon:* Supreme Court upholds Oregon state law limiting hours for women workers

1909 National Association for the Advancement of Colored People founded

1911 Bucks' Stove and Range Case: Gompers held in contempt for promoting an unlawful boycott by publishing the company's name on an "unfair" list

Triangle Waist Co. fire in New York (146 workers die) leads to establishment of New York Factory Investigating Commission

1912 U.S. Commission on Industrial Relations set up (final report, 1916)

Textile strike at Lawrence, Mass., led by I.W.W., wins wage increases

1913 U.S. Department of Labor established

1914 Clayton Act limits use of injunctions in labor disputes

1915 La Follette Seamen's Act regulates conditions for seamen

1916 Federal Child Labor Law passed (declared unconstitutional in 1918)

Adamson Act provides eight-hour day on railroads

Gompers appointed to advise Council of National Defense

Important Dates

American Labor

1941 Ford recognizes Auto Workers

    Pearl Harbor: unions make no-strike pledge

1942 National War Labor Board establishes "Little Steel formula" for wage increases based on cost of living

1943 Roosevelt establishes Fair Employment Practices Committee to seek elimination of industrial discrimination

    Strikes cause federal take-over of mines, railroads

    Smith-Connally Act passed, restricting strikes and union political activities in wartime

1945 C.I.O. joins World Federation of Trade Unions

1946 Strike wave ends in wage increases of 18½ cents an hour. Mine Workers win health and welfare fund

1947 Taft-Hartley Act, restricting union practices, passed by Congress, reinforced by state "right-to-work" laws

1949 A.F. of L. and C.I.O. help to form International Confederation of Free Trade Unions

1949–50 C.I.O. expels eleven Communist unions

1950 Korean War: A.F. of L. and C.I.O. form United Labor Policy Committee

1952 Death of Green and Murray; George Meany becomes A.F. of L. president; Walter Reuther becomes C.I.O. president

1953 A.F. of L. and C.I.O. approve "no-raiding" pact

    A.F. of L. expels International Longshoremen's Association for corruption

1955 Ford Motors accept principle of supplementary unemployment benefits in contract with Auto Workers

1957 A.F. of L. and C.I.O. achieve merger with Meany as president

    McClellan Committee begins hearings on Improper Activities in Labor and Management Field. AFL-CIO expels Teamsters, Bakery Workers and Laundry Workers for corruption

1959 Labor-Management Reporting and Disclosure Act passed by Congress

    Steel strike begins, July 15; resumption of work under Taft-Hartley injunction, November 9

1960 Steel strike ends, January 4, after concessions by employers

Suggested Reading

Although there is plenty of scope for further research in the history of American labor, there is already a wide range of secondary material for introductory purposes. It remains true today that the most useful general survey is that by J. R. Commons and his associates, *History of Labor in the United States* (4 vols., 1918–35), which takes the story up to 1932. Professor Commons also supervised the preparation of a most valuable *Documentary History of American Industrial Society* (11 vols., 1910–11), which covers the nineteenth century up to 1880. Philip S. Foner, in his *History of the Labor Movement in the United States* (2 vols., 1947 and 1955), gives a Marxist interpretation which so far runs only to 1900. A popular one-volume history is Foster R. Dulles, *Labor in America* (1949); and a recent work is Joseph G. Rayback, *History of American Labor* (1959), which has a useful bibliography. Other helpful bibliographical aids are Ralph E. McCoy, "History of Labor and Unionism in the United States" (Institute of Labor and Industrial Relations, University of Illinois, mimeograph) and Maurice F. Neufeld, *Bibliography of American Labor Union History* (1958), though the latter is very patchy.

CHAPTER I

The outstanding work is Richard B. Morris, *Government and Labor in Early America* (1946). Also of general value are Carl

233

American Labor

Bridenbaugh, *The Colonial Craftsman* (1950), John H. Franklin, *From Slavery to Freedom* (1956), Marcus W. Jernegan, *Laboring and Dependent Classes in Colonial America, 1607–1783* (1931), and Abbot E. Smith, *Colonists in Bondage* (1947). Studies of conditions in individual colonies, too numerous to mention here, add to the picture. Two useful articles are Oscar and Mary F. Handlin, "Origins of the Southern Labor System," reprinted in Oscar Handlin, *Race and Nationality in American Life* (1947), and William Miller, "Effects of the American Revolution on Indentured Servitude," *Pennsylvania History*, VII (1940).

CHAPTER II

For developments up to 1840 we are largely dependent on the first volume of Commons' *History*, but three local studies may be mentioned: Robert Ernst, *Immigrant Life in New York City, 1825–1863* (1949), Oscar Handlin, *Boston's Immigrants* (new ed., 1959), and William A. Sullivan, *Industrial Worker in Pennsylvania, 1800–40* (1955). For the women textile workers of New England see Edith Abbott, *Women in Industry* (1910), and Hannah Josephson, *The Golden Threads* (1949). Historians have tended to exaggerate the size and social cohesiveness of "urban labor" in the Jacksonian period, but a sensible view of two important controversies may be found in Joseph Schafer, "Was the West a Safety Valve for Labor?" *Mississippi Valley Historical Review*, XXIV (1937), and Edward Pessen, "Workingmen's Movement of the Jacksonian Era," *Miss. Valley Hist. Rev.*, XLIII (1956). The outstanding work for the two decades after 1840 is Norman J. Ware, *The Industrial Worker, 1840–60* (1924). Ulrich B. Phillips' work on slavery may now be supplanted by Kenneth M. Stampp's *The Peculiar Institution* (1956).

CHAPTER III

For labor during the Civil War see Emerson D. Fite, *Social and Industrial Conditions in the North during the Civil War* (1910). For the National Labor Union see Jonathan Grossman, *William Sylvis, Pioneer of American Labor* (1945). Don D. Lescohier, *Knights of St. Crispin* (1910) and J. Walter Coleman, *Molly*

Suggested Reading

Maguire Riots (1936) deal with important topics. Much new light on the period has been thrown by Charlotte Erickson, *American Industry and the European Immigrant, 1860–1885* (1957). Rowland T. Berthoff, *British Immigrants in Industrial America* (1953) is also very useful. Norman J. Ware has dealt very ably with the Knights of Labor in his *Labor Movement in the United States, 1860–1895* (1929), but has probably been too critical of Powderly, as may be thought by readers of the latter's autobiography, *The Path I Trod* (1940). For the Negro, see W. H. Lofton, "Northern Labor and the Negro during the Civil War," *Journal of Negro History*, XXXIV (1949) and Henderson H. Donald, *The Negro Freedman* (1952). S. Rezneck, "Distress, Relief, and Discontent in the United States during the Depression of 1873–78," *Journal of Political Economy*, LVIII (1950) is also helpful.

CHAPTER IV

Lewis L. Lorwin, *The American Federation of Labor* (1933) remains the best description of its subject; but Philip Taft, in his *A.F. of L. in the Time of Gompers* (1957), has derived fresh information from Gompers' records. Gompers' autobiography, *Seventy Years of Life and Labor* (2 vols., 1925) is also useful. Lloyd Ulman's *Rise of the National Trade Union* (1955) is of general importance for union growth; more specific is Robert A. Christie, *Empire in Wood* (1956), a fascinating study of the Brotherhood of Carpenters and Joiners. Two able histories of strikes are Donald L. McMurry, *The Great Burlington Strike of 1888* (1956) and Almont Lindsey, *The Pullman Strike* (1942). Donald L. McMurry, *Coxey's Army* (1929) and Melech Epstein, *Jewish Labor in U.S.A. 1882–1914* (1950) are also of value. Bernard Mandel, "Samuel Gompers and the Negro Worker, 1886–1914," *Journal of Negro History*, XL (1955), though very hostile to Gompers, is interesting. The *Final Report* (1902) of the U.S. Industrial Commission may also be referred to.

CHAPTER V

The works of Lorwin and Taft may be supplemented by Marc Karson, *American Labor Unions and Politics, 1900–1918* (1958).

American Labor

For radical unionism, see Paul F. Brissenden, *The I.W.W.* (1919) and Vernon H. Jensen, *Heritage of Conflict* (1950), which deals with the Western Federation of Miners. For the Mine Workers, see McAlister Coleman, *Men and Coal* (1943) and Robert J. Cornell, *The Anthracite Coal Strike of 1902* (1943). For the garment industry, see Joel Seidman, *The Needle Trades* (1942). An interesting discussion of the closed shop is to be found in American Economic Association, *Papers and Proceedings, 17th Annual Meeting* (1904). Much information may also be gleaned from the eleven volumes of U.S. Commission on Industrial Relations, *Final Report and Testimony* (1916). For additional topics, see Nels Anderson, *The Hobo*, (1923); Robert H. Bremner, *From the Depths* (1956), a study of the movement for social reform; Marguerite Green, *National Civic Federation and the American Labor Movement, 1900–1925* (1956); and David A. Shannon, *Socialist Party of America* (1955).

CHAPTER VI

For labor in wartime see Gordon S. Watkins, *Labor Problems and Labor Administration in the United States during the World War* (1919). For the 1919 steel strike, see the Interchurch World Movement *Report on the Steel Strike of 1919* (1920). The A.F. of L. may again be studied in the books by Lorwin and Taft, but from 1924, the latter's second volume, *The A.F. of L. from the Death of Gompers to the Merger* (1959), carries on the story. See also James O. Morris, "The A.F. of L. in the 1920's: A Strategy of Defense," *Industrial and Labor Relations Review*, XI (1956). Problems of the movement in a wider sense are dealt with in the following: J. B. S. Hardman (ed.), *American Labor Dynamics* (1928); Milton J. Nadworny, *Scientific Management and the Unions* (1956); David J. Saposs, *Left Wing Unionism* (1926); and Joel Seidman, *The Yellow Dog Contract* (1932). For labor during the depression see Broadus Mitchell, *Depression Decade* (1947), and Nels Anderson, *Men on the Move* (1940). Sterling D. Spero and Abram L. Harris, *The Black Worker* (1931) is important.

CHAPTER VII

For the New Deal period, the most useful work is *Labor and the New Deal* (1957), edited by Milton Derber and Edwin Young.

Suggested Reading

For the war period, of equal value is Joel Seidman, *American Labor from Defense to Reconversion* (1953). The enactment of the Wagner Act is dealt with in Irving Bernstein, *New Deal Collective Bargaining Policy* (1950) and its operation in Robert R. R. Brooks, *Unions of Their Own Choosing* (1939), and Harry A. Millis and Emily C. Brown, *From the Wagner Act to Taft-Hartley* (1950). Frances Perkins, *The Roosevelt I Knew* (1946) throws much light on the motivation of both political and industrial leaders. For the early history of the C.I.O. see Edward Levinson, *Labor on the March* (1938). Though good union histories are rare, the following are helpful: Robert R. R. Brooks, *As Steel Goes* (1940); Irving Howe and B. J. Widick, *The U. A. W. and Walter Reuther* (1949); and Harold S. Roberts, *The Rubber Workers* (1944). Important biographies are: Max D. Danish, *The World of David Dubinsky* (1957); Matthew Josephson, *Sidney Hillman* (1952); and James A. Wechsler, *Labor Baron: A Portrait of John L. Lewis* (1944). A more general study of union officials is C. Wright Mills, *The New Men of Power* (1948). Negro attitudes to the unions in this period are dealt with in Horace R. Cayton and George S. Mitchell, *Black Workers and the New Unions* (1939), and Herbert R. Northrup, *Organised Labor and the Negro* (1944). Three important articles are: Sidney Fine, "Origins of the United Automobile Workers, 1933–35," *Journal of Economic History*, XVIII (1948); Walter Galenson, "Unionization of the American Steel Industry," *International Review of Social History*, I (1956); and Louise Overacker, "Labor's Political Contributions," *Political Science Quarterly*, LIV (1939).

CHAPTER VIII

The works by Joel Seidman and by Millis and Brown mentioned above are of value for the early postwar period and for the passing of the Taft-Hartley Act. Max M. Kampelman, *The Communist Party and the C.I.O.* (1957) and John P. Windmuller, *American Labor and the International Labor Movement, 1940–1953* (1954) deal competently with their subjects. For the merger, see Arthur J. Goldberg, *AFL-CIO, Labor United* (1956). Corruption and racketeering are described extensively in Sidney Lens, *The Crisis of American Labor* (1959), and Lester Velie, *Labor U.S.A.* (1959);

but see also the *Interim Report* (1958) of the Senate Committee on Improper Activities in the Labor or Management Field. For a more balanced account of present-day union activities, see Jack Barbash, *The Practice of Unionism* (1956). Recent developments are discussed in two publications of the Industrial Relations Research Association, *A Decade of Industrial Relations Research* (1958) and *New Dimensions in Collective Bargaining* (1959). Also of interest is the symposium, "The Taft-Hartley Act after Ten Years," *Industrial and Labor Relations Review*, XI (1958). Charles A. Madison, *American Labor Leaders* (1950) gives interesting character sketches of Green, Murray, and others; and Robert D. Leiter, *The Teamsters Union* (1957) throws light on the structure and policies of the largest, most aggressive, and most controversial union. Fay Calkins, *The C.I.O. and the Democratic Party* (1952) shows how complex labor political action must necessarily be; and A. Kornhauser *et al.*, *When Labor Votes* (1956), reveals the unreliability of the "labor vote."

CHAPTER IX

Selig Perlman's *Theory of the Labor Movement* (1928) remains of outstanding importance among attempts to systematize the peculiarities of American and other labor movements. For effective criticism, however, see the paper by Charles A. Gulick and Melvin K. Bers, "Insight and Illusion in Perlman's Theory of the Labor Movement," *Industrial and Labor Relations Review*, VI (1953). A useful summary of this and other theories, with bibliography, will be found in Mark Perlman, *Labor Union Theories in America* (1958). On wage structure and the influence of unions, see Lloyd G. Reynolds and Cynthia Taft, *The Evolution of Wage Structure* (1956). Important works on union structure are Philip Taft, *The Structure and Government of Labor Unions* (1954); Seymour Lipset, *et. al.*, *Union Democracy: The Internal Politics of the International Typographical Union* (1956); and Richard A. Lester, *As Unions Mature* (1958). On comparative social mobility in recent years, see Seymour Lipset and Reinhard Bendix, *Social Mobility in Industrial Society* (1959). An important general study of nativism and the development of restrictions on immigration is John Higham, *Strangers in the Land* (1955).

238

Acknowledgments

I wrote most of this book during a summer at the University of Wisconsin. My first acknowledgments must be to the staffs of the two great libraries there and to the scholars and friends who made life so pleasant for me at Madison. The Provost and Fellows of The Queen's College, Oxford, gave me a term's leave of absence from teaching; a generous grant from the British Association for American Studies and the Rockefeller Foundation provided my upkeep; and a Fulbright award paid for my travel.

The text of this book has benefited much from friendly criticism. Daniel J. Boorstin has given me much valuable advice and encouragement. Jack Barbash read the whole typescript and helped me to remove errors and misinterpretations. Leon Litwack and John Laslett performed a similar service for individual chapters. I remain responsible, of course, for the errors that survive.

I obtained useful help in the choice of illustrations from Mr. A. H. Jones of the Chicago Historical Society, from Mrs. Louise Heinze of the Tamiment Institute Library, and from Mr. Saul Miller of the Department of Publications, AFL-CIO.

Index

Index

Index

Index

Index

Index

Index

Textile Workers Union, 177
Trade Union Educational League, 148
Trades Union Congress (British), 68–69, 82, 195
Trevellick, Richard, 57
Triangle Waist Company, 125
Truman, President Harry S., 179–80, 185–86, 187, 189, 194
Turner, Nat, 40
Typographical Union, International, 38, 55, 58, 70, 83, 208

United Labor Policy Committee, 196–97
United States Steel Corporation, 80, 98–99, 108, 125, 168, 186

Van Buren, President Martin, 33
Van Cleave, J. W., 108
View of the United States (Tench Coxe), 12
Voluntarism, 123, 139, 143, 152, 153–54, 160, 180

Wabash Railroad strikes (1885), 70
Wagner, Robert F., 160, 161

Wagner Act (1935), 161, 163, 167, 170, 189, 191, 205
Wagner-Lewis bill (1934), 162
Wallace, Henry A., 179–80, 193–94
War Labor Policies Board, 134
Washington, Booker T., 105
West Indies, 3, 19
Western Labor Union, 100, 110
Whitney, Eli, 25, 39
Willkie, Wendell, 172
Wilson, William B., 117, 118
Wilson, President Woodrow, 117–18, 131–32, 134, 171, 220
Window Glass Workers, 66–67
Winter, John, 16
Wisconsin Industrial Commission, 125
Women's Trade Union League, 122, 124, 162
Workingmen's Benevolent Association, 55–56
Workingmen's parties, 29–32, 61–62
Works Progress Administration, 157
World Federation of Trade Unions, 195
Wright, Frances, 30